CRIME
CONTROL
AS INDUSTRY

CRIME CONTROL AS INDUSTRY

Towards GULAGS, Western Style

Nils Christie

UNIVERSITY OF OSLO

Second and enlarged
edition 1994.

London and New York

First published in English in 1993
by Routledge
Second and enlarged edition 1994
11 New Fetter Lane, London EC4P 4EE

Simultaneously published in the USA and Canada
by Routledge
a division of Routledge, Chapman and Hall Inc.
29 West 35th Street, New York, NY 10001

Published in Norway as Kriminalitetskontroll i industrisamfunnet in 1993
by Scandinavian University Press, Oslo

Cover: Bruno Oldani
Printed in Norway by Tangen Grafiske Senter

British Library Cataloguing in Publication Data
A catalogue record for this book is available from the British Library.

Library of Congress Cataloguing in Publication Data
A catalogue record for this book is available from the Library of Congress.

ISBN 0-415-12539-1

To Ivan Illich

Preface to the second edition

Less than two years has passed since the first edition of this book went into print. Since then, the growth in prison populations within major industrialized nations has only accelerated. In Russia, a downward trend in the number of prisoners has come to an abrupt stop, and the country is back in the lead among incarcerating countries. The USA continues its extraordinary growth. In most of Western Europe also, the prison figures show a considerable increase. And everywhere more is to come. A question mark was attached to the sub-title on the first edition of this book: "Towards GULAGS, Western Style?". In this edition, I delete the question mark.

I have added a postscript to this edition. Here I describe the latest developments. In addition, numerous minor corrections and clarifications have been made.

Oslo, June 1994

N.C.

—

Contents

Chapter 1

Efficiency and decency

This book is a warning against recent developments in the field of crime control. The theme is simple. Societies of the Western type face two major problems: Wealth is everywhere unequally distributed. So is access to paid work. Both problems contain potentialities for unrest. The crime control industry is suited for coping with both. This industry provides profit and work while at the same time producing control of those who otherwise might have disturbed the social process.

Compared to most other industries, the crime control industry is in a most privileged position. There is no lack of raw-material, crime seems to be in endless supply. Endless are also the demands for the service, as well as the willingness to pay for what is seen as security. And the usual industrial questions of contamination do not appear. On the contrary, this is an industry seen as cleaning up, removing unwanted elements from the social system.

Only rarely will those working in or for any industry say that now, just now, the size is about right. Now we are big enough, we are well established, we do not want any further growth. An urge for expansion is built into industrial thinking, if for no other reason than to forestall being swallowed up by competitors. The crime control industry is no exception. But this is an industry with particular advantages, providing weapons for what is often seen as a permanent war against crime. The crime control industry is like rabbits in Australia or wild mink in Norway – there are so few natural enemies around.

Belief in being at war is one strong driving force behind the development. A general adaptation to industrialized ways of thought, organization and behaviour is another. The institution of law is in a process of change. The old-fashioned symbol was Lady Justice, blindfolded, and with scales in her hand. Her task was to balance a great number of opposing values. That task is gone. A silent revolution has taken place within the institution of law, a revolution which provides increased opportunities for growth within the control industry.

Through these developments, a situation is created where a heavy increase in the number of prisoners must be expected. This may already be observed in the USA, which in 1991 reached the up to them unheard of number of more than 1.2 million prisoners or 504 per 100,000 inhabitants. This is so high a level of prisoners that it cannot be compared to what is found in any industrialized country in the West. But why only 1.2 million? Why not two, three, or five million? And in view of the attempts to create a market-economy in the former USSR, why not a resumed use of Gulags there as well? And then, as the European welfare states decline, will these be able to resist the tempting models of the two forces now turned brothers?

But there are counter-forces in action. As will soon be documented, enormous discrepancies in prison figures exist between countries otherwise relatively similar. We are also confronted with "inexplicable" variations within the same countries over time. Prison figures may go down in periods where they according to crime statistics, economy and material conditions ought to have gone up, and they may go up where they for the same reasons ought to have gone down. Behind these "irregular" moves, we find ideas on what it is seen as right and fair to do to other beings, ideas which counteract "rational" economic-industrial solutions. The first chapters of this book document the effects of these counter-forces.

My lesson from all this is as follows: In our present situation, so extraordinarily well suited for growth, it is particularly important to realize that the size of the prison population is a normative question. We are both free and obliged to choose. Limits to the growth of the prison industry have to be man-made. We are in a situation with an urgent need for a serious discussion of how large the system of formal control can be allowed to grow. Thoughts, values, ethics – and not industrial drive – must determine the limits of control, the question of when enough is enough. The size of the prison population is a result of decisions. We are free to choose. It is only when we are not aware of this freedom that the economic/material conditions are given free reign. Crime control is an industry. But industries have to be balanced. This book is about the drive in the prison industry, but also about the counter-forces in morality.

*

Nothing said here means that protection of life, body and property is of no concern in modern society. On the contrary, living in large scale societies will sometimes mean living in settings where representatives of law and order are seen as the essential guarantee for safety. Not taking this problem seriously serves no good purpose. All modern societies will have to do something about what are generally perceived as crime problems. States have to control these problems; they have to use money, people and buildings. What follows will not be a plea for a return to a stage of social life without formal control. It is a plea for reflections on limits.

*

Behind my warning against these developments lurks a shadow from our close history. Recent studies on concentration camps and Gulags have brought us important new insights. The old questions were wrongly formulated. The problem is not: How could it happen? The problem is rather: Why does it not happen more often? And when, where and how will it happen next time?[1] Zygmunt Bauman's book (1989) *Modernity and the Holocaust is* a landmark in this thinking.

Modern systems of crime control contain certain potentialities for developing into Gulags, Western type. With the cold war brought to an end, in a situation with deep economic recession, and where the

---

1 It can rightly be said: The question is not when or where the Holocaust will happen next. It is already happening. Western industrial and financial policy results each day in death and destruction in the Third World. Nonetheless, I will in this book limit my attention to the situation within the industrial world. Crime control in the west is a microcosmos. If we understand what is happening within some of these countries, we may come closer to an understanding of Third World phenomena.

most important industrial nations have no external enemies to mobilize against, it seems not improbable that the war against the inner enemies will receive top priority according to well-established historical precedents. Gulags, Western type will not exterminate, but they have the possibility of removing from ordinary social life a major segment of potential trouble-makers for most of those persons' lives. They have the potentiality of transforming what otherwise would have been those persons' most active life-span into an existence very close to the German expression of a life not worth living. "...there is no type of nation-state in the contemporary world which is completely immune from the potentiality of being subject to totalitarian rule," says Anthony Giddens (1985, p. 309). I would like to add: The major dangers of crime in modern societies are not the crimes, but that the fight against them may lead societies towards totalitarian developments.

*

It is a deeply pessimistic analysis I here present, and as such, in contrast to what I believe is my basic attitude to much in life. It is also an analysis of particular relevance to the USA, a country I for many reasons feel close to. I have conveyed parts of my analysis to American colleagues in seminars and lectures inside and outside the USA, and I know they become unhappy. They are not necessarily disagreeing, on the contrary, but are unhappy at being seen as representatives – which they are – of a country with particular potentialities for developments like those I outline. It is of limited comfort in this situation to be assured that the chances are great that Europe may once again follow the example set by the big brother in the West.

But a warning is also an act of some optimism. A warning implies belief in possibilities for change.

*

The book is dedicated to Ivan Illich. His thoughts are behind so much of what is formulated here, and he also means much to me personally. Illich does not write on crime control as such, but he has seen the roots of what is now happening; the tools which create dependence, the knowledge captured by experts, the vulnerability of ordinary people when they are brought to believe that answers to their problems are in other peoples' heads and hands. What takes place within the field of industrialized crime control is the extreme manifestation of developments Ivan Illich has continually warned against. I include references to some of his major works in the list of literature, even though they are not directly referred to in the text. They are in it, nonetheless.[2]

Some final remarks on my intentions, and on language and form:

What here follows is an attempt to create a coherent understanding based on a wide range of phenomena most often treated separately. Several chapters might have been developed into separate books, but my interest has been to present them together and thereby open up the exploring of their interrelationships. I make an attempt to help the readers to find these interrelationships themselves, without too much enforced interpretation from me. The material I present might also be given quite different interpretations than those I have in mind. That would be fine. I do not want to create closure, enclosure, but to open up new perspectives in the endless search for meaning.

2 In addition to the intellectual debt to Ivan Illich, and to others quoted in the text, I have received important help for this book from numerous colleagues and friends. From USA, James Austin, Alvin Bronstein, Stephen Carter, Marc Mauer and Margo Picken have been particularly helpful in providing data and new ideas. In a second round with the manuscript, I have received important critiques from Bill Chambliss and Harold Pepinsky. In Canada, I have received exceptionally good help from Maeve McMahon and Ole Ingstrup. Vivian Stern has kindly helped me from the U.K., Sebastian Scheerer has helped from Germany, Louk Hulsman and René van Swaaningen have assisted from the Netherlands, while Monika Platek has provided Polish data, and also a critique of an early draft of the manuscript. From Russia, I have received valuable help from Svetlana Polubinskaya and Alexander Yakovlev, and in Hungary from Katalin Gönczöl. In Scandinavia, I have received inspiration and constructive critiques on the manuscript from Johs Andenæs, Flemming Balvig, Kjersti Ericsson, Hedda Giertsen, Cecilie Høigård, Thomas Mathiesen, Angelika Schafft, Kristin Skjørten and Lill Scherdin. The Scandinavian University Press – personified in Jon Haarberg and Anne Turner – has offered help and encouragement throughout the whole process. Peter Bilton and Anne Turner have helped my English come closer to the standards of that language, but are not to be held responsible on points where I have insisted on preserving forms and formulations I felt closer to the rhythm of my Norwegian. Berit Blindheim, Turid Eikvam, Frode Røed and Grethe Aaraas have all assisted at several stages, and June Hansen has done an exceptional job in in tidying up the manuscript. The Norwegian Non-Fiction Writers' and Translators' Association has made travelling possible during the preparation of the book.

Then on language and form: Sociological jargon is usually filled with latinized concepts and complicated sentence structures. It is as if the use of ordinary words and sentences might decrease the trust in arguments and reasoning. I detest that tradition. So little of the sociology I am fond of needs technical terms and ornate sentences. I write with my "favourite aunts" in mind, fantasy figures of ordinary people, sufficiently fond of me to give the text a try, but not to the extent of using terms and sentences made complicated to look scientific.

Chapter 2

The Eye of God

2.1 All alone

It is Sunday morning. The inner city of Oslo is as if deserted. The gates to the garden surrounding the University were locked when I arrived. So were the entrance door to the Institute and the door to my office. I am convinced I am the only living person in the whole complex. Nobody can see me. I am free from all sorts of control except the built-in ones.

Historically, this is a rather exceptional situation. Seen by nobody, except myself. It was not the life of my grandmothers, or of my mother, at least not completely. And the further back in the line I move, the more sure I am; they were never alone, they were always under surveillance. God was there. He may have been an understanding God, accepting some deviance, considering the total situation. Or He was a forgiving one. But He was always around.

So were the human products of His creation.

Towards the end of the eleventh century, the Inquisition was at work in France. Some of the unbelievably detailed protocols from the interrogations are still preserved in the Vatican, and Ladurie (1978) has used them to reconstruct life in the mountain village Montaillou from 1294 to 1324. He describes the smell, the sounds and the transparency. Dwellings were not for privacy. They were not built for it, partly due to material limitations, but also because privacy was not that important a consideration. If the Almighty saw it all, why then struggle to keep the neighbours out? This merged with an ancient tradition. The very term "private" is rooted in the latin *privare* – which is related to loss, being robbed – deprivation. I am deprived here on Sunday morning, completely alone behind the locked gates and doors of the University.

2.2 The stranger

It was in Berlin in 1903 that Georg Simmel published his famous essay on "The Stranger" – "Exkurs über den Fremden". To Simmel, the stranger was not the person who arrives today and walks off tomorrow. The stranger was the person who arrives today and stays on both tomorrow and maybe forever, but all the time with the potentiality to leave. Even if he does not go away, he has not quite abandoned the freedom in the possibility of leaving. This he knows. So do his surroundings. He is a participant, a member, but less so than other people. The surroundings do not quite have a total grip on him.

Georg Simmel would have enjoyed *Diagram 2.1-1*.

The unbroken line which hits the roof gives the number per 1,000 inhabitants of all cases of crime investigated by the police in Norway from 1956 to 1989. This is usual in most industrialized societies. In absolute numbers it is an increase from 26,000 to 237,000 cases. The other line – here, since they are so few, measured per 100,000 inhabitants rather than per 1,000 as in the line for all crimes – shows cases of crimes against honour, libel and slander, acts which are still seen as crimes in my country. As we observe, the trend here is in the opposite direction. Crimes against people's honour have gone down substantially during the last 35 years – in absolute figures from 1,100 to 700.

My interpretation is trivial. People are not more kind to each other or more careful in respecting other people's honour. The general explanation is simply that there is not so much to lose. Honour is not so important any more that one goes to the police when it is offended. Modern societies have an abundance of arrangements – intended and not so intended – which have as their end result that other people do not matter to the extent they once did. Our destiny is to be alone –

private – or surrounded by people we only know to a limited extent, if we know them at all. Or we are surrounded by people we know we can easily leave, or who will leave us with the ease of the stranger. In this situation, loss of honour does not become that important. No one will know us at our next station in life. But by that very token, our surroundings also lose some of their grip upon us, and the line for all registered crimes gets an extra upward push.

Diagram 2.1-1 All types of reported crimes investigated per 1,000 inhabitants, and slander and libel investigated per 100,000 inhabitants. Norway 1956-1991.

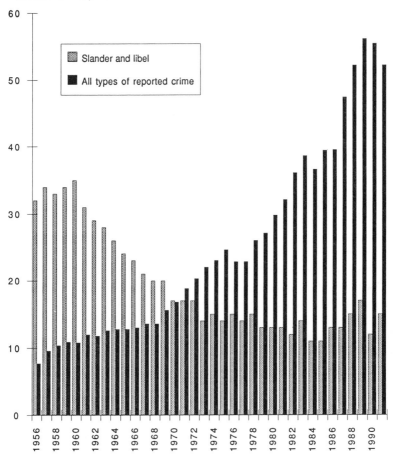

2.3 **Where crime does not exist**

One way of looking at crime is to perceive it as a sort of basic phenomenon. Certain acts are seen as inherently criminal. The extreme case
is natural crime, acts so wrong that they virtually define themselves
as crimes, or are at least regarded as crimes by all reasonable humans.
If not seen so, these are not humans. This view is probably close to
what most people intuitively feel, think, and say about serious crime.
Moses came down with the rules, Kant used natural crimes as a basis
for his legal thinking.

But systems where such views prevail also put certain *limits* to the
trend towards criminalization.

The underlying mechanism is simple. Think of children. Own children and others. Most children sometimes act in ways that according
to the law might be called crimes. Some money may disappear from a
purse. The son does not tell the truth, at least not the whole truth, as
to where he spent the evening. He beats his brother. But still, we do
not apply categories from penal law. We do not call the child a criminal and we do not call the acts, crimes.

Why?

It just does not feel right.

Why not?

Because we know too much. We know the context, the son was in
desperate need of money, he was in love for the first time, his brother
had teased him more than anybody could bear – his acts were meaningful, nothing was added by seeing them in the perspective of penal
law. And the son himself; we know him so well from thousands of
encounters. In that totality of knowledge a legal category is much too
narrow. He took that money, but we remember all the times he gene-
rously shared his money or sweets or warmth. He hit his brother, but
has more often comforted him; he lied, but is basically deeply trust-
worthy.

He is. But this is not necessarily true of the kid who just moved in across the street.

*

Acts are not, they *become.* So also with crime. Crime does not exist. Crime is created. First there are acts. Then follows a long process of giving meaning to these acts. Social distance is of particular import-ance. Distance increases the tendency to give certain acts the mea-ning of being crimes, and the persons the simplified meaning of being criminals. In other settings – family life is only one of several exam-ples – the social conditions are of a sort which creates resistance against perceiving acts as crimes and persons as criminals.

2.4 An unlimited supply of crime

In societies with limited tendencies to perceive acts as crimes, and where most potentialities for such acts are prevented by God's eye, neighbours' attendance and situational restrictions, law can be seen as a receiver of the left-over. Law becomes here a receiver of the totality of the little that has slipped through the first line of control, and has come to the attention of authorities. In this situation, there is neither room nor need for a discussion of *selection of cases.* The judges have to take what comes before them. Re-act.[1]

But as we have seen, this is not our situation. The social system has changed into one where there are fewer restraints against perceiving even minor transgressions of laws as crimes and their actors as crimi-nals. And then, at the same time, we are in a situation where the old defences against committing unwanted acts are gone, while new tech-nical forms of control have been created. God and neighbours have been replaced by the mechanical efficiency of modern forms of sur-veillance. We live in a concrete situation with crime as a mass-pheno-menon. Here anger and anxieties created from acts which also in

---

1 When they punish the offender it is not their responsibility. The responsibility rests with the person who has committed what we might call "the natural crime". Such a re-active framework – in contrast to a pro-active one – gives considerable protec-tion to those who run the system. The responsibility for what later happens is seen as resting solidly on the person who commits the crime. She/he acts, and the autho-rities are forced to re-act. The law-breaker starts it all; authorities only restore the balance.

modern societies easily might have been perceived as natural crimes, become the driving force in the fight against *all* sorts of deplorable acts. *This new situation, with an unlimited reservoir of acts which can be defined as crimes, also creates unlimited possibilities for warfare against all sorts of unwanted acts.*

With a living tradition from the period where natural crimes were the only ones, combined with an unlimited reservoir of what can be seen as crimes in modern times, the ground has been prepared. The crime control market is waiting for its entrepreneurs.

Chapter 3

Level of intended pain

3.1 Measures of pain

The amount of punishment used by the legal system in any country can be measured in several ways. I will mostly present data of imprisonment. Next to killing, imprisonment is the strongest measure of power at the disposal of the State. All of us are under some sort of restraint, forced to work to survive, forced to submit to superiors, captured in social classes or class-rooms, imprisoned in the nuclear family... But except for Capital Punishment and physical torture – measures of limited use in most of the countries discussed in this book – nothing is so total, in constraints, in degradation, and in its display of power, as is the prison.

As a measure of the use of imprisonment within a society, I will use the relative figure, that is the daily number of prisoners per 100,000 inhabitants. This is not a precise indicator, but the best we can find when we are to compare nations. Steenhuis and collaborators (1983) are critical towards this use. A low relative figure, they argue, might be the result of many prisoners with short sentences, or just a few sentenced for life. I am not convinced. Independently of the distribution between short and long sentences, it seems reasonable to say that a country with 500 prisoners per 100,000 inhabitants is one that uses measures of intended pain more than a society with 50 prisoners per 100,000 inhabitants.[1]

---

1 The number of new intakes to prison is often suggested as an indicator. This, however, leads to the problem of defining what a new intake is. To be brought into the police station, is that an intake? A stay in a waiting cell for four, eight or 24 hours,

More problematic is the interpretation of such differences. Prison figures may be seen as indicators of the crime situation of a country. This perspective is in harmony with the traditional view of natural crimes and a re-active framework. The criminal started it, the judiciary reacts. An increase in imprisonment is seen as indicating that crime has increased, while a downward trend indicates that the crime situation has changed for the better. Or, at the same historical point in time, societies with a high level of punishment are seen as having a high level of crime, while those with low levels are probably peaceful ponds in a turbulent world. This is the traditional way of interpreting the figures.

But this interpretation is not in harmony with the perspective just presented in *Chapter 2*. Here we pointed to a situation with an unlimited reservoir of acts which can be defined as crimes. This being the case, an alternative interpretation of prison figures is to see them as the end product of a myriad of influences: type of social structure, distance between people, revolutions or political upheavals, type of legal apparatus, economic interest or industrial drive. What at any particular point in time is seen as crime will certainly also play some part. It is one force, one among many. But to look at prison figures as indicators of crime, is much too narrow a perspective. And it is not in harmony with the figures that follow. Let me start at home:

3.2 The good old days?

Diagram 3.2-1 gives the prison figures per 100,000 inhabitants for Norway from 1814, the year we got our Constitution, up to the present. The diagram has the form of a huge mountain, firmly placed in the middle of the last century, followed by a low and relatively stable prison population throughout this century. The last fifteen years show a steady growth, but the relative figures have not yet reached the level of the great depression in the thirties.

---

is that to be counted? Or is it only imprisonment according to orders by the judge? In some jurisdictions, this has to take place within 24 hours. In others, the police can wait several weeks before a person is brought before the judge and his incarceration is counted as such.

The increase in the prison population from 1814 is the least difficult to explain. Leaving the eighteenth century also meant abandoning a large amount of capital punishment as well as flogging, branding a thief mark on the forehead, cutting off fingers and other mutilations. The rate of exchange prescribed for the transition from physical torment to loss of liberty was set out in an Act of 15 October 1815:

Diagram 3.2-1. Prison figures per 100,000 inhabitants Norway 1814–1991

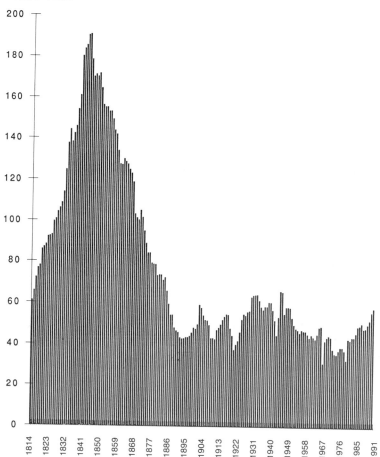

> Instead of loss of a hand, imprisonment for ten years; instead of pier-
> cing the hand and rending it, imprisonment for two years, and instead of
> piercing the hand, imprisonment for one year.

But this transition created new problems. First and foremost it caused
increased pressure on the prison system. From being one among
many forms of punishment, imprisonment now became the main
reaction to crime. Penitentiaries and other penal institutions became
full to bursting point. From 1814 to 1843, the daily number of prisoners in Norway went up from 550 to 2,325. This represented an
increase of from 61 to 179 per 100,000 of the population, or a tre-
bling in the course of thirty years. But again something happened. A
long series of amendments to the penal code from 1842 to the turn of
the century all tended in the direction of shortening the periods of
imprisonment, or avoiding imprisonment altogether. From the peak
recorded for imprisonment in 1843 it took about 60 years to return to
the level of 1814. Since then Norway has more or less maintained
this level of imprisonment.

This whole development seems to bear no close relationship to the
number of persons found guilty of crime in Norway. *Diagram 3.2-2*
gives the figures per 100,000 inhabitants from 1838 to 1991. As we

Diagram 3.2-2 Persons found guilty of crime per 100,000 inhabitants, Norway 1834–1990

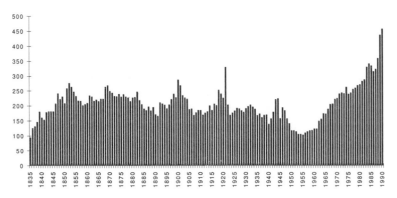

see if we compare the two diagrams, the relative number of persons found guilty remains stable during most of the nineteenth century, while the relative number of prisoners goes down to one fourth of the top level in 1844. The great increase in the number of people found guilty of crime does not start until 1960. But this does not influence prison figures until the very last years – 35 years after the increase commenced.

3.3 Europe – West

Diagram 3.3-1 is based on prison statistics from the Council of Europe. It shows prison populations per 100,000 inhabitants, mostly for 1990.

The major impression from this diagram is the extreme variation between these European nations. At the top we find the various parts of the United Kingdom. Within that Kingdom, Northern Ireland has the lead, but Scotland is not far behind. Turkey came, for a long period, close to the United Kingdom, but is now well behind. Luxembourg is now close to the top. At the other end of the diagram we find little Iceland and Cyprus, but also, surprisingly, the Netherlands. Greece comes close to the Netherlands, then Norway, Italy, the Republic of Ireland and Sweden.

For Iceland to be at the bottom seems intuitively right. It is a country beyond the reach of many influences, and has such a small population that "most people" know each other – and maybe even need each other. Honour may still count. Cyprus may be influenced by the same factors. But then comes the Netherlands, highly industrialized, densely populated, with large ethnic minorities and with drugs somewhat more easily available than elsewhere. If prison populations were seen as a measure of crime, Austria and countries higher up in the diagram would have more than twice as much crime as the Netherlands. It just cannot be.

This lack of relationship between registered crime and prison population becomes even more obvious if we move outside Western Europe.

Diagram 3.3-1 Prison figures in selected European Countries
1991. Per 100,000 inhabitants

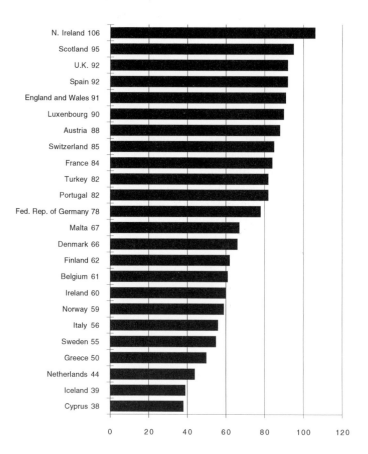

1. Source: Council of Europe: Prison Information Bulletin 1992.
2. Source: Council of Europe: Prison Information Bulletin. Figures for 1989.

3.4 Global trends

Table 3.4-1 Prison figures per 100,000 inhabitants in USSR (later Russia), Poland, Hungary, Canada and USA 1979–1991

	1979	1989	1991
USSR Russia	660	353	
Poland	300	107	
Hungary		134	
Canada	100	111	
USA	230	426	504

Table 3.4-1 shows dramatic differences between countries – and over time. In 1979, the USSR was in the lead, with 660 prisoners per 100,000 inhabitants. Poland came next, then the USA with 230 per 100,000, and then Canada at the bottom with a figure close to the norm for Great Britain.

Moving to the figures for 1989, we find the picture totally changed. In the ten years, Poland has decreased its prison population from 300 to 107, and Hungary has gone down from an unknown peak to 134.[2]

The USSR figures are particularly complicated to evaluate. I have struggled for years to get a clear picture of their size. Up until the time of the writing of this book, prison figures were still considered state secrets. As the Table shows, my estimate is that the figures have dropped from 660 in 1979 to 353 ten years later.

The basis for my estimates is as follows:

In 1979, a former prosecutor in the USSR estimated their prison figures to be 660 per 100,000. That was in a presentation that year to the American Society of Criminology.

---

2 These figures are based on estimates from colleagues in that country, particularly Monika Platek, and I have every reason to believe they are accurate. That also applies to the Hungarian figures, provided by Katalin Gönczöl from Budapest. Her estimate is that the Hungarian figures have also dropped sharply.

On a visit to Moscow in 1989, I heard from a colleague that the correct figure for that year was 214 per 100,000 inhabitants. A year later, an International Conference on Deviant Behaviour was arranged outside Moscow. Here various bits of new information emerged. The lowest estimate mentioned was 800,000 prisoners, which gave 282 prisoners per 100,000 of the population. A few months later, we had a joint Scandinavian–USSR research meeting in Sweden. Here I presented the whole spread of figures I had gathered, and asked for a sort of reaction. The answers came, mostly in body language. Extreme figures like the 1979 figure of 660 per 100,000 inhabitants were received with irritation. The suggestion of 214 per 100,000 was received with polite smiles indicating my naiveté. The figure 353 – which at that time had become my favourite estimate – was received with satisfied silence. Today, they would have told me. The Sentencing Project (Mauer 1991) suggests the figure 268 for the USSR. This is probably an underestimate.

My tentative conclusion is that the figure 353 per 100,000 inhabitants is correct for 1989. With this figure, the USSR still has an extremely high prison population according to European standards. Helsinki Watch, in a report of December 1991, confirms my estimate. Based on extensive interviews with Soviet authorities, they conclude that "the number of pretrial detainees and sentenced criminals incarcerated in the USSR amounts to a rate of 350 per 100,000 population" (p. 10). In addition, if we use this figure, there are 160,000 persons involuntarily confined in alcohol- and drug treatment institutions. If these are included, we end up with 1.1 million prisoners, or 392 incarcerated per 100,000 population.

As we see from the table, all the Eastern countries are moving towards considerably reduced prison populations. This has probably been the case in mainland China as well. Domenach (1992) has quite recently described the Gulag system of that country. His estimate is that China had some ten million people in Gulags in the early part of the 1950s, while they now are down to somewhere between 4 and 5.5 millions. On a population of a billion, this gives a prison population between 400 and 550 per 100,000 inhabitants.[3] The USSR also seems

3 Domenach in Weekendavisen, Copenhagen June 4-11, 1992.

to have had a maximum of Gulag prisoners in the early 1950s. The Academy of Science was asked in 1989 by Mr. Gorbachev to investigate the secret archives of the Ministry of the Interior. Several groups of historians were established, directed by Viktor N. Zemskov. Zemskov has published a preliminary report, available to me only indirectly (Beck 1992).[4] The major finding is that the Gulags reached their maximum in 1950 with 2.5 million prisoners. Based on the population of that time, this gives 1423 prisoners per 100,000 inhabitants. From then on, the figures declined.

But in the USA, the prison figures move in the opposite direction. The figures have risen from 230 in 1979 to 426 in 1989, according to data both from official sources and from The Sentencing Project (Mauer 1991). And the growth continues. We will come back to the US figures in Chapter 6.2. But already here: Whereas the USSR has almost cut its prison population by half during the last ten years, the USA shows exactly the opposite profile and double its incarcerated population over the very same period. Even South Africa is behind the USA with "only" 333 prisoners per 100,000 of the population (Mauer 1991). Only China is in the same category as the USA. It is of some interest to see that Canada, the closest among neighbours – according to geography, industrial pattern, language and several elements of culture – has remained relatively unaffected by what is happening in the USA with regard to the prison population. In 1989 the prison figures in Canada were 111. In 1979 they were just a bit lower. Canada keeps close to Britain, in general style as well as in what it does to those found guilty of crime. Differences in levels of crime are probably not the best explanation of this striking difference in prison figures between countries so close to each other as Canada and the United States.

3.5 The importance of thought patterns

Our data all point in the same direction: *Prison figures are of limited use as indicators of crime.* We see this from the historical perspective

---

4 For the second edition: The first major report in English is by Getty, Ritterspoon and Zemkov (1993).

in Norway. The differences in prison figures within Europe are also impossible to explain in terms of differences in what is seen as crime. A study by a group of experts from the European Council arrives at the same conclusion. The Chairman of the group, Hans Henrik Brydensholt (1982), states bluntly:

> ... there is no direct relation between the level of crime and the number of imprisonments or... number of prisoners per 100,000 inhabitants at any particular point in time.

At the global level, this becomes close to obvious. The downward trend in the prison figures in Eastern Europe cannot be the result of what is seen as the "crime situation". And more than any other figures; the enormous growth in the number of prisoners in the USA can not be a realistic reflection of changes in the crime situation of that country. Our general conclusion becomes clear: The volume of prisoners cannot be explained by what is seen as the crime level within any particular society.

Thought patterns and general theories are not impractical symbols in brains or books. They clear the way for action. The belief in prison populations as indicators of crime and the resistance this belief shows to the facts are in harmony with the old perspective from natural law, and also with ideas on what the response to such crimes ought to be. The beliefs are in harmony with reactive thinking. If the criminal starts it, and all the authorities can do is react, then, naturally, the volume of prisoners is caused by crime and reflects the crime situation. It becomes destiny, not choice.

But modern societies have at their disposal an unlimited reservoir of acts which can be defined as crimes. And we have now seen that they make very different uses of this reservoir, at least they differ in their use of one of the most important forms of delivery of pain: imprisonment. Having reached this conclusion, we are able to move on to new questions. If the volume of crime does not explain the volume of imprisonment, how can that volume then be explained? These societies have in common that they – with important variations – are highly industrialized. How come that they nonetheless are so different with regard to the use of imprisonment? How can we explain the enormous variations we have found, over time and between nations?

I will make an attempt in two stages. This is because two problems are equally fascinating. First: why do we find societies among them which make such limited use of imprisonment? And the second problem: why do we find societies in that same family of industrialized nations with more than ten times as many prisoners as others?

Let me once again start at home, or close to home, where the question will be: why do these countries have so few prisoners?

Chapter 4

Why are there so few prisoners?

4.1 Waiting for Pain

Norway has 2,500 prisoners. The numbers have stayed relatively stable this century, but are now on the increase. 2,500 out of 4.2 million inhabitants is about 58 per 100,000. This is still relatively low for a highly industrialized country. With modernity, with increased anonymity and anomie, with a steady growth in the number of crimes reported to the police, why have the figures not gone into the sky?

They have not, because we place potential prisoners on waiting lists.

We have 2,500 persons in prison. But we have 4,500 on waiting lists. We line them up and let them wait for admission.

Authorities are embarrassed. Waiting lists for kindergartens, waiting lists for hospitals, waiting lists for home nurses. And then waiting lists for the reception of pain. It can't be right.

I understand the uneasiness among the authorities, particularly when I try to explain this arrangement in England or in the United States. It is as if citizens in those countries cannot believe their ears. Waiting lists for imprisonment? It sounds somehow out of style, a dissonance, like a piece of hard Rock in the middle of Debussy.

Why?

The uneasiness is probably there because the arrangement is out of harmony with the current stereotypes, both of prisoners and of the function of prisons. We all know the basic rules in games of cops and robbers. The police have to catch the robbers, throw them into prison, and keep them there. It is a tough and dangerous job. If the bad guys get a chance, they escape. This was the game of childhood. It is the game in the media, a reality according to the script. The criminal is arrested, detained while awaiting trial, and then sent straight to prison to serve his sentence.

And it is a true description, in some severe cases. But most cases are not. So, here comes the dissonance. Most sentenced people are people, ordinary people, not a special breed, not bandits. They are to blame for something, but they are not wild animals. They can wait, we all can. The drama is gone.

The queue is out of harmony with the stereotypes.[1] Recognizing the queue is to recognize that those lined up there are not dangerous, are not monsters. They go to prison – eventually – for other purposes than the protection of the public. This forces us to reflect. That is why this arrangement is a good one. But the arrangement is also bad – for those in the queue. It is difficult to plan the future when on the waiting list. And people there are unhappy, knowing pain will come. Some remain passive, in their dwellings, as if in prison already. According to Fridhov (1988), those with former prison experience worry most about the coming stay in prison, they know what to expect. First-timers take it easier, they do not know.

Another consequence of the queue is its inhibiting effect on authorities. The Police know that there are no empty rooms in the prisons, and hold back. The judges know. In what are seen as serious cases, this does not prevent the use of imprisonment. But again, most cases are not serious.

The logical next questions are these: Why not build more prisons, or at least increase the capacity of those we already have? Most prisoners in Norway have "single rooms", that means one, and only one

---

1 Waiting for trial is quite another matter than waiting for being punished. When waiting for trial, the game goes on according to the script, not contrary to it.

person for each cell. There are exceptions with bigger rooms built for several inmates, but not many. With two persons in each cell, most of the waiting list would vanish within a few years. This became clear to the authorities, and they decided to double up a number of the single cells.

A coalition of two forces has up till now blocked such a possibility. First, the prison guards. The labour movement is a strong one. The guards are unionized, with considerable political influence. They also guard their own working conditions. They are strongly opposed to running prisons above capacity. At a meeting for all their elected leaders (Landsstyret) in 1990, they made a formal declaration where they stated they were:

> strongly opposed to the decision of having two inmates in rooms built for one person and point to the following negative consequences:
>
> It is not acceptable from a security point of view.
>
> The working conditions for the guards will deteriorate.
>
> It is not acceptable to let prisoners live below decent health- and social standards.[2]

They write letters to the Law Committee in Parliament, they arrange meetings with politicians, they stand close to the party which most of

---

2 This is more than conventional argument for the occasion. In 1989, the same organization, and similar ones in Denmark, Finland, Iceland and Sweden, agreed on a set of ethical rules for prison guards. These state:

> Inmates do not consist of any homogeneous group. They have, however, regardless of what sort of crime they have committed, the same need as all other people for being respected as human beings. The fact that many among them have committed serious crimes, makes it necessary to meet them with a joint attitude built on the role of the experienced worker within the field. A basic trait in this role is the common ethically based attitude. This again is based on respect for the worth of each human being.
> Those sentenced to imprisonment must not be caused unnecessary suffering. A guard must not behave in a way which unnecessarily degrades the inmate or those close to the inmate.

the time has ruled the country. The prison authorities stuck for a while to the decision to double up some cells, but for mysterious reasons this repeatedly proved impossible. Health authorities also protested against this deterioration of living conditions. A new minister of justice reversed the decision, and the principle of one person to a cell has been preserved.[3]

The guards would probably not have succeeded were it not for two other forces working in the same direction: Most prisoners strongly dislike the idea of sharing cells, and the liberal opposition is against it. But such voices are traditionally weak. Why are they listened to here?

To explain that, we have to move to the mountains.

Every year, just after Christmas, a peculiar meeting takes place somewhere in the Norwegian mountains. By now it has become a sort of tradition, after having taken place twenty times. The meeting is held in a hotel of fairly high repute, with two hundred people participating for two nights and three days.

Five groups are there:

First: Official operators of the penal law system, prison directors, guards, doctors, social workers, probation officers, prison teachers, judges, police.

Second: Politicians. Members of the Storting (the Legislative Assembly), sometimes Ministers, always advisers of some sort, and local politicians.

---

3 The importance of this fight for preservation of the principle of one person for one cell is put in perspective by a description of British conditions (Stern 1987, p.6):

In 1966 Lord Mountbatten said: "It should be more widely known than it is that there are still thousands of prisoners sleeping three in a cell designed in the nineteenth century for one man". More than twenty years later things are no better. In these very same cells, built over a hundred years ago for one person, 5,000 prisoners are living three to a cell and nearly 14,000 are living two to a cell.

Third: the "liberal opposition", lay people interested in criminal policy, students, defence lawyers, university teachers.

Fourth: People from the media.

Fifth: Prisoners, often people still serving sentences, but on leave for these days. Some arrive in cars from their prisons and in the company of staff from these prisons. Others are temporarily released and arrive by ordinary bus. Not everyone is given leave of absence from prison to participate. Inmates regarded as very likely to escape would not be let out. But there are often participants serving for serious crimes: murder, drugs, armed robbery, espionage. During late evenings and nights one can see – if one happens to know who is who – prisoners, prison directors, guards, policemen and representatives of the liberal opposition in heated discussions on penal policy in general and on prison conditions in particular. But they can also be found in relaxed and peaceful talks on the prospects for the next day's cross country skiing.[4]

An important effect of these meetings is to include prisoners in the joint moral community of the decision makers. Norway is a small country. Those with responsibility for running the formal system of crime control cannot avoid knowing each other, or at least of each other. They cannot escape their critics, and the critics cannot escape those with responsibility. We are forced into some degree of proximity. The situation does not lend itself to complete distortion. One may have strong feelings of animosity, but often with some doubts somewhere. Maybe the other party has a point. A peculiar feature is

---

4 The meetings are arranged by the KROM, an organization for crime reform. They have now gone on for 25 years, largely owing to the initiative and energy of Thomas Mathiesen (1974, 1990). For most of the period, Mathiesen was the chairman. Mathiesen has particularly emphasized the need for keeping such an organization to a middle course, to keep a distance from both the most radical political movements and the establishment. Central in this attempt has been the acceptance of "the unfinished" as a valuable condition:

Contradiction to and competition with the old society lie in the very unfolding of 'the alternative society'. Contradiction to and competition with the old society lies in the very inception and growth of the new ... The alternative society, then, lies in the very development of the new, not in its completion. Completion, or the process of finishing, implies a full take-over, and there is no longer any contradiction. Neither is there competition. (Mathiesen 1974, p.17)

that most of the officials are graduates in law. They are old students of their even older critics. Pictures of monsters do not thrive under such conditions.

But this is too idyllic a description. The participants are a select sample. Some upholders of stern law and strict order would not dream of participating up there in the mountains. But a sufficient number from all sections are there to create communication. A sufficient number are there to leak into the system a fundamental doubt as to the productivity of more prisons, as well as some doubts about the usefulness of the trend in Europe in general and in the United States in particular.

This is not limited to the mountains. It also happens within the universities, where practitioners are often invited. And it happens within the framework of the Scandinavian Research Council for Criminology, which regularly arranges joint seminars for practitioners and researchers in various areas.

A general effect of all these meeting places has probably been to establish some kind of informal minimum standards for what is considered decent to do in the name of punishment, and also that these standards are valid for *all* human beings. Why the standards are as they are, is close to impossible to explain. I will make an attempt in *Chapter 11* on *Crime Control as Culture.* But concerning their validity for all people, let me suggest here, as a minimum, that this has something to do with imaginative power, the capacity to see oneself in the other person's situation. In the contrasting situation, with the offender seen as another breed, a non-person, a thing, there are no limits to possible atrocities. Cohen (1992 p. 12) describes one type of justification of torture used in modern Israel: "… and after all, they don't really feel it, look at the violence they inflict on each other." In public debates one often hears: "It hurts more for the better situated to be in prison."

Identification makes general standards valid for all, and functions thereby as a prevention of more extreme measures. It could have been me, found guilty, brought to prison. Identification creates the very situation Rawls (1972) constructs as an instrument to create just solutions to various conflicts. It is a situation where the decision-makers do not know which party they belong to in a conflict. Coming close to culprits has much the same effect. It invites all sorts of inhibitions. Mentally, the judge acts, in the words of Rawls, under the veil of ignorance. He is brought close to the culprit. He might have been him. He has to decide with care.

Jessica Mitford (1974, p. 13) quotes *The New Yorker*'s Talk of the Town column after the Attica uprising:

> ... millions of Americans were brought face to face with convicted criminals for the first time. Most of us were wholly unprepared for what we saw ... The crowd we saw on television was not a mob but a purposeful gathering, and the men we saw were not brutalized, although they may have suffered brutality – they were unmistakably whole men ... acting with dignity.

Again, this must not be exaggerated. The joint moral community is under increasing strain. A brief look at the other main instance of low prison figures in Europe shows the vulnerability in the situation.

4.2 Tolerance from above

That little country of the Netherlands, densely populated, highly industrialized, with great religious and ethnic divisions, and nevertheless has had – until recently – one of the smallest prison populations in Europe. It is a mystery. And this low level has been one of the important arguments in the European debate on the necessity of prisons. If the Netherlands can make it, why not also the rest of Europe?

Louk Hulsman (1974) described the level of leniency at the point in time where the number of prisoners was close to its bottom:

> ... the decline in the prison population is attributable not to a drop in the number of custodial sentences imposed but solely to a reduction of their duration. Their relative briefness and the continuing trend to shorten them still further may perhaps be termed the principal characteristic of recent Dutch penal developments. Only thirty-five sentences of three years or more were passed in 1970, of which fourteen were for homi-

cide (though sixty-three persons were convicted of that crime in that year), two for rape (total number of convictions: sixty-eight), thirteen for robbery with violence, and the remaining six for burglary in combination with extortion ... Parole is almost invariably granted and is not conditional upon the prisoner's willingness to participate in rehabilitation programs (p. 14).

David Downes (1988) described some of the mechanisms which made this possible. The Netherlands had suffered war and occupation. Several of the leading academicians experienced life as prisoners. They came out of it with a strong conviction of the negative effects of imprisonment. There were many teachers of penal law among them. These became teachers of the danger of severe prison sentences. This has penetrated the whole penal establishment, not least the police, as many representatives of law and order visiting the Netherlands have experienced.

But in Belgium and France, leading academicians were also imprisoned during the Second World War. They, too, had their bad experiences. Yet the prison figures in their countries have not been visibly reduced as a result. Why is there this difference?

David Downes points to the tradition of tolerance in the Netherlands. Louk Hulsman (1974) agrees and uses the weighthouse of Oudewater near Gouda as a symbol for it. At the time of the great witch-hunts in seventeenth-century Europe, people came from near and far to Oudewater to prove that they were not weightless, – as witches at that time were supposed to be. In Oudewater they got a certificate of weight, safeguarding them from prosecution both there and elsewhere. Rutherford (1984, p. 137) quotes a source from 1770 stating that more criminals are executed in London in a year than there have been in all Holland for twenty years.

In addition to tolerance, comes a peculiar Dutch mechanism for coping with conflicts. The history of that country is filled with external as well as internal conflicts. The people have learned to live with their internal differences. They have learned the art of compromise. One mechanism to escape conflict has been to delegate decision-making up to the top of the system. Here representatives of opposing forces in Dutch society are given the mandate to sort out their differences and come up with solutions that can be lived with by all the various parties. It is an undemocratic solution, but preferable to civil war at the local level. Crime control has been organized according to the same principles. The Dutch have no lay judges. It is a highly professionalized system. Representatives of law and order have been given the mandate to cope with crime policy according to their own views of what is necessary. That has given them extraordinary powers. With the experience of the Second World War in mind, they have used this power to resist the expansion of the crime control industry.

But they were not alone. The Parliament was behind them. According to Hulsman (1974):

> The debate in the Dutch parliament on the Ministry of Justice budget for 1947 was of unusual interest in that a clear majority urged the government to reconsider its basic position with regard to the penal question. The majority view being that the penal system constitutes a social problem in itself, the government was requested to prepare a concrete plan for tackling this fundamental matter.

But a system based on tolerance from above is a vulnerable one. As David Downes points out (p.74):

> The major price, so to speak, for such an arrangement is that the élites, both in and outside government and Parliament, are relatively insulated from criticism, unless in exceptional circumstances.

And now these exceptional circumstances seem to have gone. The Netherlands is on the move. The development in numbers per 100,000 inhabitants since 1880 is presented in *Diagram 4.2-1,* which also includes figures from England and Wales. We can see that both lines have a downward direction from the end of the last century. Behind the British trend was Winston Churchill. Rutherford (1984, p. 125–126) quotes him from the House of Commons:

> We must not allow optimism or hope, or benevolence in these matters to carry us too far. We must not forget that when every material improvement has been effected in prisons, when the temperature has been rightly adjusted, when the proper food to maintain health and strength has been given, when the doctors, chaplains, and prison visitors have come and gone, the convict stands deprived of everything that a free man calls life.

Diagram 4.2-1 Prison population: Average daily rate per 100,000 inhabitants, 1877–1985 (excluding offenders detained in mental institutions and Dutch state labour colonies) [1]

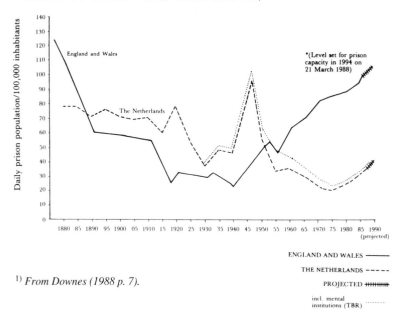

[1] *From Downes (1988 p. 7).*

This was remembered up to World War II. Then England starts its race towards the European championship in incarceration, while the Netherlands continues its low course until quite recently. But now this seems to have come to an end. The figures are on their way up again.

What has happened?

Certainly the Netherlands has been under extraordinary international pressure to change its drug policy in a more severe direction; Germany and Sweden in particular have long claimed that the Netherlands is the weak link in the drug defence of Europe. Although David Downes shows that this is not quite true, the pressure may nonetheless have affected penal policy. The situation may have been experienced as an embarrassment to the experts within the establishment. As in all other European countries, these experts become increasingly linked to their opposite numbers in the international system, and may slowly be brought to share their frame of reference.

The Dutch representatives become personal objects of the international irritation caused by their drug policy.

The country is adapting to European standards in other aspects, too. The old divisions have faded away. This probably makes it less important to give a mandate to those at the top to solve all sorts of problems in isolation from the population. Crime policy becomes less of a matter for experts, the mass media start to interfere, and demands on the politicians from the general population are more strongly felt. The old divisions dissolve and make room for new, this time divisions between ordinary people and those seen as criminals.

Another factor is the de-escalation of welfare-benefits. Hulsman lists with pride several of these benefits in his 1974 article, and claims that they are behind the exceptional mildness of the Dutch system. Today, (oral communication) he explains the increased severity by the absence of several of these benefits.

Worth mentioning are also two developments related to the universities of the Netherlands. A generation of law professors has been replaced; the veterans have left their chairs, taking with them their personal influence and their experience from having been imprisoned. Changes have also taken place in criminology. The Netherlands was the stronghold of criminology in Europe. Most universities had chairs in criminology, or their chairs in penal law were filled with people whose major interests lay in criminology. The criminology of the Netherlands was also of a peculiar kind. It was a critical criminology, more interested in raising questions than in giving answers of immediate use to the authorities. It was also a criminology with exceptionally strong links to humanistic and cultural activities. According to van Swaaningen, Blad and van Loon (1992), several of the criminologists were rather successful novelists or poets. Recently, this whole tradition has sharply declined in the Netherlands. Chairs in criminology have been left empty, and whole institutes have been abolished. Instead, research close to government has grown rapidly. At the ministerial research and documentation centre, there are at present as many criminologists employed as at all the universities together. It is difficult to know if this development is an effect or a cause of what is happening in the penal area.

The latest news from the Netherlands is sad news, for those who liked that country as it once was. The daily number of prisoners for the first months of 1992 is about 7,600, which means 52 per 100,000 inhabitants. If the growth continues, the number will reach 62 per 100,000 in 1995. In 1975, the prison figures were – according to Rutherford (1984, p. 137) – 2,356 prisoners, which then meant 17 per 100,000 of the population. The Netherlands has tripled its prison population since 1975, and Europe has lost its most spectacular case of tolerance.

4.3 Between East and West in Europe

Finland was, for a long period, the land of incarceration among the Nordic countries. *Diagram 4.3-1* gives the general picture[5]. Three trends are visible:

First, the initial similarity in the developments up till 1918. We find the same sharp rise in the prison population in the first part of the last century in Finland as in the other Nordic countries, and we get the same decline later on. Finland was at that time a part of Russia, but not with regard to pain-delivery.

But then comes the deviation. In 1918, the Finnish figures suddenly jump to 250 prisoners per 100,000 inhabitants. Later they fluctuate for a long time around 200 prisoners per 100,000 inhabitants, while compared with Finland the prison populations in the other Nordic countries are stabilized at quite a modest level between 50 and 100 per 100,000 inhabitants.

The third development is the recent decline in the Finnish figures, illustrated in *Diagram 4.3-2*. Here is shown the development from

5 Figures for the imprisoned collaborators with the German occupants after the Second World War are omitted for Norway. The Finnish figures do not extend further back than to 1886. This was just before the deportations to Siberia came to a halt. Altogether 3,236 Finnish prisoners were deported during the period 1826 – 1888. Figures for Norway are a bit too low in the beginning, since persons sentenced to work in the fisheries in the far North (or for females to work in the households up there), are not included. The Swedish figures are too low since some administrative decisions are not included.

Diagram 4.3-1 Prisoners per 100,000 inhabitants in Scandinavia
1887–1987

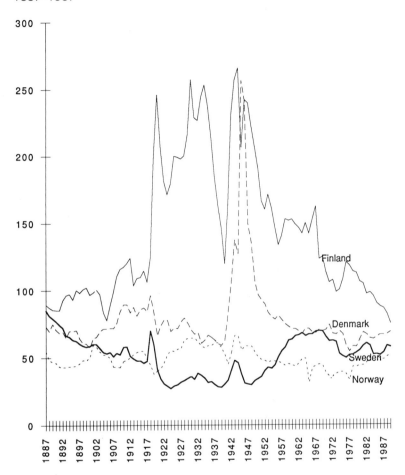

1965 to 1990. As of 1991, the total number of prisoners went even further down, to 2,427, which means that Finland that year had 49 prisoners per 100,000 inhabitants. From being at the top in the use of
imprisonment – even according to general European standards – they
are now close to the bottom.

Diagram 4.3-2 The number of prisoners in Finland 1965–1990

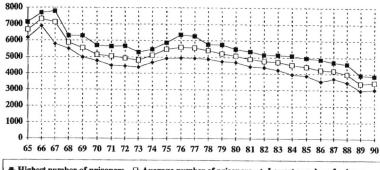

Source: K-J.Lång (1989b)

Seen in a national-political perspective, these three stages are rather paradoxical. From 1809, Finland was a part of Russia, but her penal policy was Nordic. From 1919, she got her independence, but left the Nordic family and became much more punitive. But then, in the last stage, she has by-passed all Nordic countries in limiting the use of imprisonment.

But moving closer to history, we get some clues. I shall focus on the development from 1918. The dramatic *increase* from that year is the most simple to explain. 1918 was the year of the war of independence, followed by an unbelievably fierce civil war. 8,000 of the losers in that civil war were executed immediately afterwards, and an additional 10,000 perished in the prison camps. This major cleavage in the population remained all the way up to the internal unity created by the two wars against the USSR, first in 1939–40 and then from 1941 to 1944. Finland got accustomed to a level of pain and suffering far beyond the usual Nordic standards.

K.J. Lång is the director general of the prison system in Finland. Among the Nordic countries, he is the one with the longest time in that service. He expresses no illusions regarding the reasons for the high prison figures (Lång 1989a, pp. 83–84.):

... the number of prisoners has very little to do with crime. The number of prisoners is rather caused by the general situation of confidence in society and of the political equilibrium. The political turbulence during three wars, the right-wing movements of the 1930's and the criminalized communist movement (of that time), have all led to a greater use of imprisonment in Finland than in any other Nordic country...The legislation has meant that we got accustomed to a high punitive level with long sentences for the various crimes. .. Finland had throughout the 1970's three times as many prisoners as Norway. Not because Finland put three times as many persons in prison, but because each prisoner was kept in prison about three times as long in Finland as in Norway.

But then comes the question of the decline. What is behind the recent dramatic decrease in the use of imprisonment in Finland? One reason for the decline may be that the reasons for the high level have gone. But that is not necessarily enough as an explanation. Social conditions tend to remain, out of tradition or vested interests. What is, is, because it is. But something happened in Finland. Patrik Tørnudd (1991) descibes it. He points to a unique combination of historical antecedents, ideological constellations and also hard work by a number of dedicated individuals.

First of all, according to Tørnudd, it is a question of perceiving a problem as a problem. To do so, it was necessary to become aware of the fact that Finland's prisoner rate was exceptionally high. It was also necessary to understand that this was not caused by an unusual crime profile in Finland. And lastly, it was necessary to reject any attempt to see the high number of prisoners as something to be proud of, e.g. as indicators of the determination and toughness of the criminal justice system or of its readiness to spend its resources on prolonged rehabilitating efforts and on the protection of the public.

According to Tørnudd, professional criminologists provided the necessary data. They documented that Finland was out of line with the rest of the Nordic countries in size of prison population, and they refuted the popular explanations for this – that crime in Finland was so different from crime in the other Nordic countries. But this would not have been sufficient to bring down the prison population. Not only were experts providing essential information, they were also in positions to change conditions. Tørnudd writes (p. 5–6):

> ... the Nordic countries can generally be characterized as fairly expert-orientated, and Finland has been said to be the most expert-orientated among the Scandinavian countries. Certainly it is true that crime control never has been a central political issue in election campaigns in Finland.
>
> ...
>
> But the fact that it became possible to carry out a large number of reforms aimed at reducing the level of punishment was ultimately dependent on the fact that the small group of experts who were in charge of reform planning or who worked as crime control experts in research institutes and universities shared an almost unanimous conviction that Finland`s internationally high prisoner rate was a disgrace and that it would be possible to significantly reduce the amount and length of prison sentences without serious repercussions on the crime situation.

Tørnudd concludes (p. 13):

> The decisive factor in Finland was the attitudinal readiness of the civil servants, the judiciary and the prison authorities to use all available means in order to bring down the number of prisoners. Through the efforts of a group of key individuals it had become possible to define Finland's prisoner rate as a problem and that problem conception in turn produced a number of activities, ranging from law reforms to low-level day-to-day decisions, which all contributed to the end result.

> As the background of the efforts to reduce the Finnish prison population had its unique antecedents, there are no guarantees that present trends will continue. During the last year prisoner figures have fluctuated upwards.

Tørnudd's concern seems to be well founded. There are interesting similarities between Finland and the Netherlands. In both cases, the low prison figures seem to be a result of acts carried out by a centrally placed elite. But that sort of power is vulnerable. In addition, dark clouds have recently appeared over Finland. With the breakdown of the USSR, Finland's economy is badly hurt. In this situation, it is not improbable that her prison figures will once more show an increase. Those working for a decreased number of prisoners were successful in a situation of full employment and material progress. The test of their accomplishments will be when the carriers of these ideas are out of their positions, and the material conditions of the nation are changed. This is what is just about to happen.

4.4 Welfare states at the brink

The situation in the old welfare states is one of unstable equilibrium. Most resistant against destruction are probably the countries with relatively stable economies, long traditions as welfare states and small and homogeneous populations. Affluence provides scope for tolerance, tradition makes it less offensive to share, and small and homogeneous populations create inhibitions against excluding people in perceived need. It also helps to stabilize an unstable situation if the society recognizes several different criteria for goals in life, and has some regard for the "poor but pure", or for generosity rather than efficiency.

But homogeneous small-scale states are also under pressure. They are having to use more money on welfare. *Table 4.4-1* illustrates developments in Norway from 1970 to 1990. In the 16 to 49 age-group, the number of persons on pensions due to some sort of disability has increased from 26,400 to 63,800. This does not mean that people are more sick in 1990, but that there is a greater need to be defined as disabled, and thereby be entitled to aid or assistance. Even more people have been recipients of general social welfare, with an increase from 21,500 to 141,000. 10–15 percent of these may also have received disability pensions. In the same period, and for the same age-group, registered unemployment has increased from 20,000 to 99,000. These are the concrete problems. Aggravating them is the fact that the welfare states, too, are troubled by all the organizational principles forced on them by industrialization. Growth takes place in the centres, division of labour becomes a necessity, insurance compa-

Table 4.4-1 Strains on welfare

Age 16–49	1970	1975	1980	1985	1988	1990
Disability Pensioners	26 400	30 400	34 400	44 100	55 300	63 800
Receivers of Social Care	21 500	33 200	45 900	87 500	121 800	141 000
Unemployed	20 000	34 000	30 000	48 000	62 000	99 000

From Breivik (1991)

nies replace mutual aid, and impersonal relations play a greater part. These developments erode much of the moral basis of the welfare principles. At the same time, these changes are also among the driving forces behind the steady increase in the amount of crime registered by the authorities. They are also behind the decrease in reports on crimes against honour.

In this new situation, even the most established among welfare states face temptations. Temptation to protect themselves, or the agencies for social service, rather than those in need.

Several major lines of defence have been drawn up. One is within social welfare itself. Some social workers create more distance between themselves and those in need of welfare. Some workers at municipal social service centres protect themselves against their clients; they keep the centres open for applicants only a few days a week, and on those days only at certain hours every morning, so that people in need line up from 5 a.m. to get access. Telephones are not answered, private police patrol the premises, ordinary police are called in if the social workers feel threatened, as they of course are likely to, given the unfamiliarity created by this distance to their clients. These lines of defence can be found, but only as exceptions.

Another line of defence is to get potential trouble-makers away from ordinary people and into segregated areas. The most extreme example of this is about to be built in Sweden. In the town of Ørebro they had for a long time struggled with the problem of untidy and noisy tenants in their apartment houses. It was seen as unfair for these people to be allowed to create disturbances for the ordinary people living in the buildings. But now the municipal authorities have come up with a solution. The largest newspaper in Sweden, Dagens Nyheter, ran this story on September 28, 1991:

> In Ørebro, plans have been prepared for a secluded living area for particularly disturbed and disturbing tenants. Fireproof floors, walls and roofs, outer doors made of steel, other doors strengthened to be able to resist a kick by boots, and small windows high up on the walls.
> …
> The municipality has worked almost three years on these plans. They call it protected living quarters. Steel bunkers is what their critics call it.

...

The floor must be able to resist a forgotten cigarette without setting the whole house on fire. Doors must be able to resist attacks. The tenants often bring with them a tail of more or less violent visitors. And nobody living there should risk an axe through his entrance door as punishment for an unpaid liquor-debt from the night before, says Torgny Larsson, social worker with the unit for adult abusers in the social service of Ørebro.

...

Only ten years ago, this would have been impossible, and triggered an outcry about social ghettos, he says. And certainly we have to show solidarity in our housing policy. But there are limits. I find it unacceptable for a disturbing person to be allowed in the name of solidarity to break down a whole block for ordinary decent people.

With this type of building, welfare states are rather close to creating their own prisons. But of course, there is a difference. The tenants of Ørebro would still be free to sleep under the bridges rather than in the municipal steel cages, at least if they were able to do so without being observed by municipal authorities or police.

Additional problems are created by the so called "de-institutionalization" movement. Particularly, this is a movement bound to exert pressure on the level of prisoners in these welfare states in the future. The trend here, like everywhere else, is towards "normalization". Mental institutions and special schools have been abolished. The slogan is "back to normality". This may have two consequences. Some extraordinary people may be unable to cope, and therefore end up in prison. But another aspect is also important. De-institutionalization does not mean that the institutions disappear. They remain, empty, and their former staff remain, empty-handed. This creates both a pressure and a temptation. Some of these buildings can easily be converted into prisons, and the staff into prison officers. Just now a war is raging in Norway around the site for a new so-called "health prison" for "particularly deviant prisoners".[6] These are not seen as insane, but as so deviant that highly qualified experts are needed. Such experts are rare. They live in or close to the big cities, in the south of the country. But the empty houses and empty hands are on the West Coast. A new place for warehousing is ready. It is all a reproduction

6 *Dagbladet* Nov 11 and Nov 15, 1991

of Foucault's (1967) story of the leprosy houses from Medieval times being converted into hospitals for the mad.

Even the general educational system wants to sell out to the prison service these days. Parts of the education system are in need of more pupils. This is particularly true of some "Folk High Schools", residential schools mostly situated in the countryside. In Norway, one of them is run by the DNT, a branch of The International Good Templars, an organization based on total abstinence from alcohol. But also the applicants are drying out, so now the teetotallers are offering the whole school – for rent or sale – to the Ministry of Justice as an open prison. To keep to their heritage, they want the place used as a special prison for drunken drivers and they therefore suggest that:

> the Ministry of Justice rent the place and ask the DNT to run it according to clearly defined guide-lines and with the prison service as the responsible inspectorate.
> …
> We feel responsibility for those now working at the place, and guarantee that they are responsible and good employees.
>
> The DNT is a humanitarian organization. For 130 years we have worked to distribute information on the dangers of intoxicating substances, particularly alcohol. We do not represent private profit interests, but are concerned with providing a useful and meaningful service to society.
> …
> Some within the DNT would be concerned if Sunny Hill was called a "prison". We believe in open prisons … For that reason, we propose that the place be called: *Sunny Hill – expiation and study-centre.*

We like this slogan:

Expiation with meaning.

Scandinavia has neither private prisons, nor entrepreneurs fighting to get them. But when potential student or welfare money disappears, the old instruments from welfare and education are there, ready to be used for new purposes. The left-overs from welfare as well as from idealistic humanitarian organizations become a sort of functional alternative to the more direct push from private capitalistic interests which will be described in *Chapter 7*. With the decrease in international tensions, military camps will also become emptied and invite new users. The military industry, particularly in electronics, will also eagerly look for new fields of application.

4.5 Will it last?

The low punitive level in these archetypes of welfare states is threatened by several forces. Some are of a general character. They have to do with effects of industrialization, the labour market, and national conflicts. They will be considered in the next chapters. But some are specifically linked to developments in or close to the institution of penal law. These forces will be discussed in what now follows.

My first point is that the joint moral community among those responsible for the penal policy in these countries is under severe strain. 1968 and the student revolt meant a certain democratization. It meant greater attention given to the rights of certain groups among the weak and the vulnerable. But at the very same time it also meant increased influence at all levels of the penal establishment. As a part of the general democratization, these practitioners create their own labour organizations and pressure groups vis-á-vis the political authorities. The prison officers in Norway have blocked the trend towards two in each cell, but are lobbying for more prisons. The police organizations are also working for expansion. A century back they were the mute tools of politicians. Conditions have improved, and deteriorated.

Internationalization is another strain on the low level of pain-delivery. Also in the old days, cosmopoliticians were active. Lombroso and Ferri from Italy, and later von Lizt from Germany were well known figures in the Nordic debates. As Naucke (1982) and Radzinowicz (1991b) have documented, the stated goals for the International Association of Criminal Policy, and the ideas of von Lizt in particular, contained germs of what after 1933 developed in Germany. The effects of these ideas on Scandinavia are unclear. The general decline in prison figures comes to an end at the turn of the century. It might have ended without help from abroad. One major result of the various international contacts was the creation of several types of so called "special measures" of enforced treatment or education, or long time internment of those supposed to be non-improvable. It has taken most of a century to get rid of the majority of these measures.

To day, internationalization has moved downwards, to the practitioners in prisons, the probation service, and the police. Increasingly, these practitioners relate to their peers abroad, acquire reference groups in the big and tough countries, obtain information on how the world "really is", and can more easily shrug off criticism from the "theoreticians" whom they see as living their "unreal" lives in ivory towers.

A further strain on the values which keep the prison figures low is created by the penetration of management ideology into the state administration. The old personnel saw themselves as civil servants with a major obligation towards a complex set of rules. Often enough, they were caricatured as disappearing behind mountains of documents, slow, but reliable. With management orientation, simplified goals of concrete results and productivity are gaining more weight. A large number of persons "Waiting for Pain" might in some quarters be interpreted as a clear sign of inefficiency. Also within the Scandinavian bureaucracies can be seen what Feeley (1991b) calls "the new penology" with a focus on management of aggregate populations. The management ideology is also invading the universities. From the top, the university-administration demands planning, efficiency and reports of goals reached. And from the bottom, the students demand useful knowledge, that is knowledge their coming masters – the managers within state and business – will demand from them. This means that the old university standards of critical thinking come under strain. Students become more interested in being equipped with answers that solve administrative problems than with critical questions which only complicate the tasks of those with administrative responsibilities. The moral power of the question-makers is thus diminished.

The future is unclear. Maybe countries with exceptionally few prisoners will gravitate towards the level common to so many industrialized countries. A great deal depends on the more general developments within the industrialized world.

Chapter 5

Control of the dangerous classes

Place: A large industrial town somewhere in Europe.

Time: A day in September, pleasant, sunny, not warm, not cold, ideally suited just to hang around. Which was exactly what so many did most of that day. Not in pubs or coffee-places, but on street corners, close to parking lots, or they gathered on some of the empty fields where old houses had been demolished and no new ones had been raised.

Colour: Grey. The sun was out, but was not real. People were grey. The houses were grey, dust and litter and misery reigned the arena.

Most of those hanging around were unemployed. That was the reason for their presence.

Coming from one of these protected corners of the continent where unemployment had not yet hit – this was some time back in time – I had to control what I knew was my naive urge: To buy 1000 large brooms and thereafter organize a festival for cleaning up the place and the atmosphere. One broom to each man, for they were mostly men – the females were at home caring for house and children – and then we could have wiped away some of the greyness, the dust, the dirt, the misery.

But of course, I knew this was naiveté, and did not do it. I knew that unemployment has nothing to do with lack of tasks in urgent need of being done. Unemployment does not mean lack of work, it means lack of paid work. Unemployment is an organizational problem – one with severe social consequences. It is a question of distribution of the entrance ticket to what in these cultures is seen as a major symbol of full membership. It is a question of power to be able to obtain the ticket, or solidarity in sharing tickets.

This competition for the status of paid work is softened by several mechanisms. Postponed entrance to the labour market, mostly through compulsory education, makes it legitimate to keep youth in consumer roles. Ideas of life-long learning also keep people out of competition for paid work. Early retirement or liberal use of the criterion "bad health" are other honourable ways out of the rank of paid workers. These mechanisms can all provide means for consumption without a head-on collision with the norms of consumption as a result of production.

5.1 The surplus population

The "empty hands" have been a problem since the earliest stage of industrialization. All those drifting around were seen as creating at least two types of trouble: the one by its potentiality for unrest, the other through the dissonance between this enforced lifestyle of unemployment and the official morality of industriousness. The unemployed might come under suspicion of enjoying their destiny. To both problems, houses for "forced labour" represented a solution. But this solution was only a temporary one; the states were poor, the labour houses had to be based on private capital, and profit was greater in other types of investments. In Europe, emigration to the USA relieved much of the pressure. The workhouses were abolished. And lastly, stated in all its brutality, two world wars also gave periodic relief.

But the basic problem has not gone. On the contrary, new categories are demanding access to what is seen as a full life. Females are moving back into the market for paid work – just where they were in the beginning of industrialization. With the same quota of the population wanting paid work in 1992 as in 1965, there would not have been any "unemployment" in countries like Denmark and Norway. Justice for females in societies organized like ours creates complications for lower class males.

In addition comes what is now happening in Eastern Europe. With all the defects of the old regimes, they nonetheless had a strength in not accepting unemployment. It was, under the old regime, seen as a prime responsibility for the state to guarantee that paid work was available to all able to work. A non-productive idea, probably. We have all heard stories about over-staffed Eastern factories and offices. But all the same, this was an arrangement which hindered unemployment. It meant a guarantee of the right to share one of the most important tools for dignity between humans. Uneconomical, wasteful, open to fraud and corruption – but still a guarantee; participation in the work-process was for all.

With this old system gone, Eastern Europe is getting Western problems. At the very same time, the most extreme forms of Western belief systems on the advantage of free competition and letting the market decide increase their hegemonial grip. There seems to be no alternative. Work was shared in the East. That went wrong. Shared work might be dangerous. We are left with the surplus population, those outside production. And we are left with the classical problem: How to control the dangerous classes? How to control all those who are no longer controlled by work-mates, and who might find it unjust to remain outside the important and dignity-creating activity of production? How to control those who, in addition to all this, are also forced to experience considerably lower material standards than those in ordinary work?

5.2 Stocks in life

In the days when the eye of God was supposed to see everything, there were also built into the system benefits for good behaviour. Life did not end at death, rewards or punishments might follow. Even lifestyle might count. Matthew, Chapter 5, verse 3, has this to say:

> Blessed are the poor in spirit, for theirs is the kingdom of Heaven.

Some translations even state it more strongly:

> Blessed are the poor, for theirs is the kingdom of Heaven.

Theologians disagree on the choice between these two translations. The first one is at present the official one. But the second is by far the more powerful when it comes to social control. Here all the poor get their reward, eventually. Such a society does not necessarily get in trouble with its surplus population. That population can be kept waiting, poor but honest.

But that society is not our society. Ours is founded on a considerable amount of talk about equality in this life, and of dissatisfaction when it becomes clear that this talk is just talk. So, we have to resort to other forms of control.

A basic tenet of social control is that those who own very much and those who own nothing are the two extremes that are most difficult to govern. This is so because those who own much also have much power, and those with little, have nothing to lose. They have no stocks in life, no property, maybe not even a social network and thus not even honour. This is what Jongman (1991) calls a theory of bonds. Jongman gives fascinating data from the Dutch town of Groningen. In the thirties, unemployment was high, and today this is being repeated. In both epochs, the work-load on the police increased. And in both periods, the researchers were able to show that unemployment is of major importance. And increasingly so. What seems to happen is that the legitimacy of inequality is weakened. In periods close to full employment, the few without paid work might easily see themselves – and be seen by others – as deficient. Their unemployment is their own fault. With mass-unemployment, the feeling of guilt fades.[1] It becomes natural to look at unemployment as created by society, and put blame in that direction. Jock Young (1989, p. 154) has an important critique of earlier epochs' understanding of poverty:

---

[1] This seems to be the case also in the complex social fabric of the US. For a review-article see Freeman (1983)

The failure of the social democratic consensus of the 1950s that better conditions would reduce crime was based on notions of the reduction of absolute deprivation. But it is not absolute but relative deprivation which causes crime (Lea and Young 1984). It is not the absolute level of wealth, but resources perceived as unfairly distributed which affects the crime rate.

And Young continues with a prescription for crime-prevention which sounds like a list of steps *not* taken in modern welfare states these last years:

To reduce crime we must reduce relative deprivation by ensuring that meaningful work is provided at fair wages, by providing decent housing which people are proud to live in, by ensuring that leisure facilities are available on a universal basis, and by insisting that policing is equally within the rule of law, both for working class and middle class, for blacks and for whites.

Balvig (1990, p. 25) points to the basic problem as one of non-usefulness. The message in the development is that there is no longer any reason to trust that the welfare state will provide work for all. Society is gradually changing from having a shared – common – rationality into one of individual rationality.

5.3 Drug control as class control

For the police, as for most people, the situation offers no easy answers. The number of reports to the police is increasing rapidly in most industrialized nations. Some call it crime, some call it complaints. Either way, behind it are acts from nuisances to severe dangers and suffering among people who see no other solution than to address the complaints to the police. But in reality the police can do very little. The quantity of commodities that can be stolen is steadily increasing. There is so much to remove, so much to drink. There are too few people around in the living quarters in the daytime, and too many in the entertainment quarter at night. People do not know each other. The police have no magic available. With an exception for grave cases of violence where all resources are mobilized, they can in such a society solve little more than what is solved

by itself. This creates a crisis in State hegemony, says Philippe
Robert (1989, p. 109–110):

> In fact, since the victim usually cannot identify the offender, what else
> can he or she do but file a complaint? Recourse to the criminal justice
> system is no longer an element in a strategy; it has become an automatic
> process for which there is no alternative.
> … police action is increasingly half-hearted, since there is no known
> suspect in most complaints and, as everyone knows, this means that
> there is hardly any chance of the police solving the case.

It was in this situation the war on drugs appeared and created alternative possibilities for control of the dangerous population. But let me
add. Behind this view is no theory of conspiracy. There are several
rational arguments behind the wish for some sort of control of both
imports and use of drugs, even though the means applied can be dis-
puted. That the war against drugs also provides an opportunity to
control the dangerous classes in general does not discredit either the
original motives, or the central persons in the drug war. Consequences
are different from reasons.

A salary for doing nothing is to some extent in dissonance with our
usual work ethic. Why would anybody apply for unpleasant work if
welfare benefits are close to the level of the lowest salaries? A double
provocation is built in if those who are paid for doing nothing use this
money for bad purposes, particularly for what are seen as criminal
hedonistic purposes. First, they get the money without having had to
provide the labour. Second, they get illegal pleasures without any
effort.

In addition comes the basic negative view of drugs among many of
the founders of the welfare state. Particularly at the beginning of the
war against drugs in Scandinavia, we still believed that we had made
it. We had full employment, free education, free medical services,
and a general belief in steady progress. Those who so wished, could
work their way into the good, deserved life. But then came drugs.
The hippies arrived, and rejected some of the fruits of affluence.
After the hippies came the drop-outs of all sorts. Two interpretations
were possible. Maybe there were still defects in the welfare system.
Maybe industrialization – even in welfare states – meant losses to

some people. And maybe old social injustices had remained, and the drop-outs represented the old losers in a new form. The alternative interpretation was that the danger lay in the drugs. Drugs were actually so dangerous that they destroyed people even in the most perfect of welfare societies.

It is easy to see which answer was most suitable for those responsible for building the welfare state. A war against drugs was declared. And such a war was not in contrast to welfare, but in harmony with it. One element of welfare is to care for people, care for them even against their own wishes, and also to protect the vulnerable against the dangers in life. This can easily lead to coercive treatment of those regarded as in need, and to harsh penal measures against those regarded as a danger to the rest of the population.

A war against drugs was also in harmony with the strong old tradition of teetotalism in several of the Scandinavian countries. But the war against liquor had been lost. That was an additional reason for being stern on other drugs. But here Norway and The Netherlands have taken different roads. The Netherlands – with quite a different alcohol tradition from Norway – has only to a limited extent gone into the drug war – to the great irritation of the leading warriors elsewhere in Europe.

But Norway has gone into it. The country has been one of the most uncompromising fighters against illegal drugs. This policy has to an extreme extent relied on penal measures. Up to 1964 the maximum penalty in drug cases was 6 months of imprisonment. After 1964, sentences could reach what was at that time considered the very high level of 2 years of imprisonment. But then the development accelerated; in 1968, the maximum could be 6 years; in 1972, 10 years; in 1981, 15 years; and in 1984, the ceiling was reached at 21 years in prison which is the most severe sentence possible in Norway.

Wars often have unexpected gains, as well as unexpected costs. A general cost of the war against drugs has been that people have fallen for the easy solution; had it not been for drugs, social conditions would have been so much better. When poverty is explained by drugs, it is not necessary to take up a more serious discussion of the failures of welfare arrangements. An additional expense has been the lack of attention to alcohol problems. In the shadow of the war against drugs, drinking has taken on more severe forms.

The unexpected advances – from the point of view of those who see what now follows as advantageous – are of another type. The war against drugs has to a large extent become a repetition of what Gusfield (1963) describes from the Prohibition period. The crusade at that time was directed not only against alcohol, but also against new pretenders to the moral hegemony in the USA. In all industrialized societies, the war against drugs has developed into a war which concretely strengthens control by the state over the potentially dangerous classes. They are not challengers, as described by Gusfield, but offensive in lifestyle. Not only are hedonism deplored and shortcomings in society explained (away), but also, quite concretely, a large segment of the non-productive population is securely placed behind bars. Much of the unbelievably rapid increase in the prison population in the USA stems from the stricter laws and practice against illegal drugs. Much of the severe strain on European prisons stems from the same war against drugs.

The effects on Norway of these developments over the last ten years are reflected in *Table 5.3-1*. What I have done here is simply (less simply in practice, though) to count how many years of imprisonment the judges have handed down for each year since 1979. As we can read from the table, they have nearly doubled the volume of intended years of pain in these ten years: from 1,620 to 3,022. The next column reveals how much of this is for drug sentences. Here we can see that the increase is from 219 to 789 years; that means nearly a fourfold increase in ten years. And lastly, we can see that drugs played an increasingly important part in the pain-budget up to 1983. A quarter of all years of intended pain are now for drugs.

The overall impression given is that the increase in the use of punishment in Norway in the last ten-year period – in terms of the number of sentences and of sentence severity – is primarily due to drug-related developments. Particularly in extremely long prison sentences, drug related crimes are predominant. This is even evident in the way the official statistics are presented. In previous years, our traditions

Table 5.3-1 Number of years of imprisonment decided by the courts each year in Norway from 1979 to 1990. Total number, and number for drugs.

Year	Total	Drugs	Percent drugs of total
1979	1620	219	14
1980	1630	245	15
1981	1792	326	18
1982	2073	388	19
1983	2619	650	25
1984	2843	684	24
1985	2522	592	24
1986	2337	458	20
1987	2586	683	26
1988	2688	756	29
1989	3022	832	28
1990	3199	789	25

were such that three years of imprisonment was regarded as extremely long. Such sentences were correspondingly rare. The statistics gave an impression of this, specifying sentences in the smaller units of days and months. But when it came to taking years from people's lives, the Central Bureau of Statistics felt that a simple division of 1–3 years would do, and then a combined category for the very few cases of more than 3 years. This was sufficient, up to and including the statistics for 1986. But then the combined category overflowed and was split up into 3–4, 5–6, 7–8, 9–10, 11–12, 13–14 years and 15 years and over. It is particularly in the areas of 3–8 years that narcotics offences constitute the bulk of cases.

But it is not only at this heavy end of crime control that drugs become the road into the system. Also at the light end, drugs become important. The supposedly dangerous population is attacked on two fronts. Some of them are seen as importers of drugs, professionals are what they are often called. But they are also defined – and they are often the same people – as a threat to good order, and for that reason subjected to coercive measures.

With the recent downward trend in the economy, drug abuse becomes a particularly tempting invitation to certain forms of penal control. The increased unemployment is reflected in an increased quota of people on skid row. Poverty has again become visible. The homeless and the unemployed are out in the streets. They hang around everywhere, dirty, abusive, provocative in their non-usefulness. We get a repetition of what happened in the thirties, only more so since the inner cities have been rebuilt since then. Hiding places in slums and dark corners have been replaced by heated arcades leading into glittering shopping paradises. Of course, homeless and/or unemployed persons also seek these public alternatives to the places of work and homes they are barred from. And as an equal matter of course they are met with agitated demands to get them out of sight and out of mind. Back in the thirties, this was accomplished by seeing similar categories as "sick" and in need of treatment. A special prison was built, where people arrested for drunkenness in the streets were warehoused for long periods of time under the pretext of treatment for alcohol-problems. Similar arrangements existed both in Finland and Sweden. In the 1960s and the 1970s this was all abolished. Today, newcomers among the unwanted are again seen as sick or at least without ordinary will-power due to their supposedly irresistible demand for drugs. And now these categories are even more suited for penal action. In the thirties, their sickness was seen as related to alcohol, after all a legal substance and used by the majority. Only abuse could be punished, not use. To-day, all use is abuse. The illegality creates a clear-cut difference between "them" and "us".

The ground for increased use of coercive measures against drug-users has been prepared by several other developments:

The gaps between classes, even in welfare states run by social democrats, are clearly widening. The number of extremely rich people is going up, while the living standard of the population in general is sliding down hill. This creates a need to keep one's distance from the bottom. In the thirties, those at the bottom also represented the bottom of the working class. To day, they are in a sense below the ordinary scale, and it seems reasonable to change the terminology, from class to caste. HIV and AIDS are over-represented among heavy drug users. This is well known, and creates both disgust and anxiety. These people are in effect gravitating towards the status of untouchables. In the public debate, it has been suggested that all carriers of HIV ought to have a tattoo on their body, telling the truth. In the old days, bells were fastened to lepers, to warn that they were coming. In the field of social control, radically new inventions are seldom introduced.[2]

But it is not quite right to say that these untouchables have moved from class-status into one of caste. The situation is worse. In traditional caste societies, members of the lowest castes are met with extreme forms of discrimination. They are forced to keep their distance from the more privileged ones. But there are limits to disadvantages. Members of the the lower castes are of use to the rest of the system by carrying out necessary, but extremely low regarded work. Through their acts, they make it possible for the pure castes to remain pure. In this lies a certain protection. The junkies are below that sort of usefulness, and therefore also without the protection of being needed. Their primary usefulness is that they provide examples of unwanted conditions, and raw-material for the control industry. Being socially distant and creating disgust and fear, they are in a highly vulnerable position.

The war against drugs has in practice paved the way for a war against persons perceived as the least useful and potentially most dangerous parts of the population, those whom Spitzer (1977) calls social junk, but who actually are seen as more dangerous than junk. They illustrate that everything is not quite as it should be in the social fabric, and at the same time they are a potential source of unrest. In Spitzer's terminology, they become junk and dynamite at the very same time. Through the war against drugs, a pincers movement encircles them. For some of their acts, they are seen as serious criminals. They are called "drug-sharks" and are incarcerated for exceptionally long periods if they import or sell more than minimal amounts of drugs. In reality, most of those thus punished are themselves users, situated at a considerable distance from the top of society (Bødal l982). The large-scale dealers from the middle- and upper classes do exist, even in the prisons, but as rare exceptions. On the other side of the pincers move-

---

2 Lill Sherdin has been particularly helpful in a discussion on this question. I have also here profited from her thesis (Sherdin 1990).

ment, we see initiatives to establish coercive cures. In this connection, largely the same people are now seen more as miserable misfits. Between the two sides of the pincers movement, they are caught in a firm grip.

5.4 Fortress Europe, Western division

This book is being written during one of the most turbulent periods in the history of modern Europe. As I write, the USSR is coming to an end. So is the iron curtain. At the northern tip of my country, we have a common border with what is now Russia. Without any iron curtain, we have to face the new realities of that neighbourhood.

We do not like everything we see.

It is particularly uncomfortable to get such a clear picture of poverty. Those living close to the border react as good neighbours. They invite hungry people in, or collect food to send. But at the state level, it looks different. Russia is so big; what if all those people, or even a fraction of them, got the idea of going west? Those hungry neighbours would certainly eat us out of the house. 2.5 million adults have already decided to go west according to an EEC-study of January 1992. An additional 10.5 million say they will probably decide to go.[3]

The problem is similar in countries further down the map. It is the same all around Western Europe. We are surrounded by hungry neighbours. And the solution is clear; the old fence created by Stalin and his likes must be raised once more, and now also extended to the south. Africa is also hungry. And so is Asia. Fortress Europe is taking shape, Fortress Europe, Western Division.

The ground had already been prepared before the USSR dissolved. Several steps had been taken. The first is symbolised by the letters TREVI. This is an intergovernmental forum for the Interior and For-

3 *Aftenposten*, January 1992, p. 3.

eign Ministers of the European Community. The group has also given the status of observers to certain other countries, like the United States, Canada, Morocco and the Nordic countries. TREVI stands for **T**errorism, **R**adicalism, **E**xtremism and **V**iolence. The group was set up in 1976, principally to combat terrorism, but the original mandate has since been extended to special groups on "Police Cooperation", "Serious Crime and Drug Trafficking", and, last but not least, "Policy and Security Implications of the Single European Market".

The legal framework for these operations is to a large extent established in *the Schengen Agreement.* Schengen is a town in Luxembourg, where that country, together with France, West Germany, Belgium and the Netherlands in 1985 signed a formal agreement to abolish their internal border controls ahead of the rest of the European Community. It was seen as a pilot project for the new community. After much disagreement, and criticism of the extreme amount of secrecy surrounding the agreement, a detailed Convention was signed in June 1990. Here Italy, Spain and Portugal also joined. In the words of Abel et al. (1991, p. 4):

> while yet to be ratified, its provisions on police cooperation and information exchange are the most detailed insight we have on the shape of things to come.

And things to come are all in defence of Fortress Europe.

First, the police will be able to cross borders between countries. They will be entitled to carry their own firearms, but entry into private homes and places not accessible to the public is prohibited.

Second, a joint information system will be established.(Convention, Art. 92):

> The Schengen Information System shall enable the authorities designated by the Contracting Parties, by means of an automated search procedure, to have access to reports on persons and objects for the purposes of border checks and controls and other police and customs checks carried out within the country...

New technical tools will also soon be available for this control. In a
new criminal justice newsletter, Europe (vol 1 number 1, p. 3) we are
told:

> Researchers at Essex University in England are experimenting with a
> fingerprint scanning system that can be coupled with a credit card to
> reduce fraud. A model of the device is being tested by a company
> owned by the University, Essex Electronic Consultants, to resolve pro-
> blems associated with the device.
> ...
> A scanner at the business location would be used to compare the credit
> card bearer's fingerprint image with the one embedded in the card's
> magnetic strip. In addition to its use to prevent credit card fraud, the
> technique is believed to have many more applications, including cash
> machines, drivers' licenses, passports and personal identification.

And third, a tight system of control of foreigners has been established. The external borders can only be crossed at authorized crossing-
points. The states will carry out a common policy with regard to
people outside fortress Europe. They will harmonize policies on visa
and asylum requests, and exchange information on those seen as not
wanted. Entrance can be denied if other "Schengen-countries" have
negative information on a person. "A no from one country, is a no
from twelve. A yes from one, is a yes only from one" (Morén 1991,
p. 43). The company carrying anybody across the border can be fined
if that person is without valid documents. Great Britain has applied
this rule for two years now, at a cost to the carriers of 11 million
pounds sterling.

What does this all add up to ?

A sort of siege. Internal borders are being weakened, but this is com-
pensated for by strengthened internal control in the form of armed
police with authority to cross national borders and a shared information system; and, as the essential element, a much more efficient system of control at the external borders. The iron curtain is down, up
comes the Visa curtain.

Maybe Western Europe at least for some time to come will be able to
preserve a relatively low level of prisoners by keeping what will be
seen as the most dangerous elements outside this assembly of affluent

CONTROL OF THE DANGEROUS CLASSES **73**

societies. Maybe Western Europe for a while can be preserved as an island of welfare by locking the poor out, rather than locking them into the prisons of the Fortress. By waging a war against the foreigners, we might also become less preoccupied by the fight against those traditionally perceived as the internal enemies. The question is only whether the price for this much wanted prison-situation may be too high. Let these last reflections protect us against European self-satisfaction when, in the next chapters, we look into what is happening on the other side of the Atlantic.

5.5 Money in slaves

To have slaves was, in certain periods, a profitable arrangement. This century has seen several successes. Stalin's work-camps and Hitler's concentration camps fulfilled numerous tasks. When they went out of use, it was not because they did not achieve what they were designed for. Even up to the last stages of the old regimes in Eastern Europe, several of the prison systems were run at a profit. Work morale was low both inside and outside of prison, but much easier to control inside. I remember a visit to a model prison in Poland before democratization. From the top floor there were factories as far as the eye could see. These factories were all inside a massive wall, and belonged to the prison. According to the vice-director of the prison administration for the whole country, the system as a whole was run at a considerable profit. To-day, that profit has probably gone. But not everywhere. The Helsinki Watch (1991, p. 36) has this to say after a long and detailed study of Prison Conditions in the Soviet Union:

> Prisoners receive a wage from which is deducted money to pay for their upkeep. They can perform services for the colony, such as cleaning, cooking, maintenance or providing medical care (if they are properly qualified) or else they can work in the production facility of the camp. Timber, furniture-making, metalworking, and simple electronics are some of the industries found in the colonies. Prison production is sold to the general public and was until recently exported to "fraternal socialist countries." It is unclear how the export of prison products has been affected by the downfall of most communist governments in Eastern Europe and by a reorientation of Soviet trading relations toward hard currency transactions, but one press report noted an effort by prisons to

enter into joint ventures with Western European firms. Prison production is a vital part of the Soviet economy, accounting for 8.5 billion rubles of revenue per year. In 1989, profits from prison production amounted to 1.14 billion. In some areas, prisons are monopoly producers, particularly in agricultural machinery.

The situation is similar in China. Domenach estimates in an interview[4] that China exports goods worth some 100 million dollars each year from their Gulags. He finds this less deplorable than other conditions related to the Gulags. To get the work done, it is necessary to treat the prisoners with a minimum of dignity and also to see to it that their material standards do not deteriorate too badly. With this observation, we are back to our reflections on the difference between caste and class. Being important for the economy, prisoners move slightly up in the hierarchy. They get at least some importance. That also means a degree of power. This could mean trouble ahead for authorities.

5.6 Traces of a future

The prospects for the distant future will be the theme in *Chapters 11 and 12*. But already here it may prove useful tentatively to suggest some possible lines of development. These suggestions will not be the final ones. They just serve as a device for creating some order in the house before we embark on a somewhat more extensive description of industrialization in general, and the situation in the USA in particular.

One preliminary suggestion is related to the Finnish-Dutch-Norwegian model. They are welfare states at the brink, for reasons we have described. It is far from certain they will be able to preserve their profile. But there are some signs that these models may be rescued, and even strengthened, by developments in other European nations. Prison figures in both Germany and in Great Britain are on the way down. A conscious pro-active policy is sometimes expressed, and often economically motivated as prisons become too expensive. And

4 Weekendavisen, Copenhagen June 4-11, 1992 & L' Evénement du Jeudi

there are spokesmen for this direction. In Great Britain, Rutherford (1984) is a leading advocate for what he calls a reductionist agenda. Of central importance in this agenda is the proposal that the physical capacity of the prison system should simply be substantially reduced – down to 50 percent is his suggestion:

> The reductionist target for the early l990s should not be around 52,000 as planned by the Home Office, but 22,000 or, in terms of the prison population rate per l00,000 inhabitants, not 110 but in the region of 35.

In quite a recent book, *Growing Out of Crime*, Rutherford (1992) documents a drastic decrease in the use of imprisonment for the very young offenders in England and Wales.

Disbelief in prisons in Europe has also been stimulated by Mathiesen's book *Prison on Trial. A Critical Assessment* (1990). The traditional arguments for imprisonment are analyzed and refuted, and we are instead presented with radical alternatives to imprisonment. The books by Rutherford and Mathiesen, and they are not the only ones, exemplify cultural views that are still valid in Western Europe. The most radical alternative to penal law has been the writings – and even more the teaching – of Louk Hulsman from Rotterdam. His major theme has been attempts to bring unwanted acts from the domain of penal law over to civil law. In harmony with this approach, he describes penal law not as a solution, but as a social problem in itself.Thus, the goal is not only to limit the use of imprisonment, but to abolish penal law altogether. Or, in the words of another Dutchman, Willem de Haan (1991):

> Abolitionism (what this tradition of thinking is often called. N.C.) is based on the moral conviction that social life should not and, in fact, cannot be regulated effectively by criminal law and that, therefore, the role of the criminal justice system should be drastically reduced … (p. 203).

> … This is not to deny that there are all sorts of unfortunate events, more or less serious troubles or conflicts which can result in suffering, harm or damage to a greater or lesser degree. These troubles are to be taken seriously, of course, but not as 'crimes' and, in any case, they should not be dealt with by means of criminal law (p. 208).

But there are also indicators pointing in the opposite direction. The developments in Eastern Europe are of great importance. The immediate effects of Glasnost and all that followed was the strong reduction in prison figures we observed in Chapter 3. But Glasnost also meant an opening for preoccupation with crime in the mass-media. From being a taboo-theme, it became the same type of entertainment-theme as in the West. And that in a social situation where there is every reason to fear social unrest, and where the prison system still plays a major economic role for the state. As formulated in a report by the Helsinki Watch (1991, p. 36):[5]

> With colony labor so valuable to the Soviet economy, the pressure against meaningful reform of the penal system is great. Decreasing the number of prisoners sentenced to labour colonies, decreasing their sentences, increasing their pay or emphasizing rehabilitation in the labor system all run counter to the goals of production and profit. Upsetting the economics of the labor colonies means upsetting the economy as a whole, adding more severe stress to an economy that is contracting and on the brink of hyperinflation. Reform of the work system thus requires serious political commitment at the highest level.

There are no signs that such a commitment is alive. On the contrary, the pressures on the shaky government's structure are for more law and order. Crime control can be seen as a useful arena for showing strength, particularly when the show can be run with a profit. The last officially published figures on number of persons sentenced to imprisonment in the USSR are not promising. *Table 5.6-1* shows the expected decrease from 1986 to 1988, but then they move up again in 1989 and 1990. That year was the end for the USSR, but Russian colleagues suggest that the increase has continued in their country in 1991 and 1992 as well. Gilinsky (1992) documents that the number of sentenced persons who receive imprisonment steadily has increased since 1987.

5 Helsinki Watch is a part of Human Rights Watch. This is an organization composed of five Watch Committeees: Africa Watch, Americas Watch, Asia Watch, Helsinki Watch and Midde East Watch and the Fund for free Expression. In Chapter 6.4 we will quote from their report on conditions in US prisons.

Table 5.6-1 Number of persons sentenced to imprisonment in the
USSR 1989–1990*

1986	45 8729
1987	30 5495
1988	23 1767
1989	24 4785
1990	29 2992

* Statistical Collection: Crimes and other offences in the USSR 1990, Moscow 1991.

But again there are at least potentialities for changes. With Perestroika and Glasnost come ideas of protest. The pre-trial detention centers within Russia and the other states in the old USSR are just horrible. Helsinki Watch (1991) has this to say about living conditions there (pp. 14–15):

> Conditions in the pretrial detention centers are appalling. Those we saw were all overcrowded, airless, hot in summer, cold in winter and usually smelly. Butyrskaia in Moscow, originally built hundreds of years ago as a fortress, has a capacity of 3,500.[6] On June 11, 1991, when we visited, it had 4,100 inmates, of which some 250–300 were convicted criminals with pending appeals. Krasnopresneskaia, with a capacity of 2,000, always has 2,200–2,300; when we visited it had 2,264. "Two hundred sixty-four have no place to sleep," the prison chief told us, "and must sleep either sideways or on the floor." The notorious Kresty detention center, the larger of two serving the 5 million people in the Petersburg area, has a capacity of 3,300 but a population of 6,000–6,500! "The further one gets from Moscow," one official told us, "the worse things get".

A team from the Danish newspaper Politiken[7] confirms the report from the Kresty prison in St. Petersburg. Kresty means cross, and this seems suitable as a metaphor for a prison with up to 14 inmates in cells of eight square metres.

6 Since 10-15 percent of a prison's cells are usually under repair or used for other than regular housing, the actual capacity is closer to 3,000.
7 Politiken, Copenhagen, May 10, 1992

> My whole body hurts because I can never stretch my legs or back, said a tall, young lad. He was the last arrival, and had therefore to sleep close to the door and the open toilet.

Or again in the words of Helsinki Watch (p. 15):

> Inmates sit or lie on their beds, often bent over if on the bottom bunk. The windows are shut, or if they are open, they are so blocked by metal bars or blinds that no light or air gets in. The doors are solid, with only a peephole or sometimes a slot through which food can be passed. Ventilation is virtually nonexistent; the cells are hot in the summer and cold in winter, and are often only dimly lit.

Prison authorities are desperate, but see few possibilities for reform. "I know how a prison ought to be," said the director to the journalists. "I have been on a study-tour to Finland. But to us, such conditions are just a dream."

The question is only how long the director and his staff will be able to keep control. There have been several cases of violence against guards in Kresty. In February 1992, two guards were kept hostage, one killed. The Helsinki Watch (1991 p. 22) reports that riots and hostage-taking have become more and more common. Here is their list:

> ■ October 1991 – Grozny pretrial detention center – 600 prisoners riot. Two dead after uprising put down by force. Detainee complaints:unknown.

> ■ July 1991 – Novokuznetskii pretrial detention center – 400 detainees on hunger strike. Detainee complaints: poor ventilation, inadequate medical care, limited food in commissary, harsh treatment by guards.

> ■ August 1990 – Krasnodarskii krai, Armavirskii pretrial detention center no. 2 – 200 participate in hunger strike. Detainee complaints: poor food, lack of cigarettes, poor health care, overcrowded cells.

> ■ June 1990 – Dnepropetrovskaia pretrial detention center – Uprising of more than 2,000 detainees – rioting, arson. Riot put down by special forces storming the facility. Five detainees died; accounts differ as to responsibility of troops for deaths. Detainee complaints: overcrowding, poor medical and other living conditions.

The pre-trial prisons are the worst, and for that reason particularly threatened by unrest. The Colonies are generally better places to live. But also here trouble may lie ahead. Prisoners will know they are important to the system, important as producers. They will slowly raise demands for improved living conditions and for a share of the profit. Slaves will come closer to the position of workers. And now a new situation arises since the system is somewhat more open to Western ideas. This will probably increase their bargaining power.

Even in the Chinese Gulags, changes seem to take place these days. Domenach has an interesting observation. He describes the Chinese control system within the prisons as detailed in the extreme. The slightest deviance, a sigh at the wrong time or place, and someone may register that the person is on the wrong path. Perfect is only the prisoner who knows the official ideology by heart, and also the wishes of the authorities before they are formulated. To reach this goal, an elaborate system is constructed with extremely detailed mutual control within all small groups where prisoners are members. Here there is no need for the eye of God. The group members see all, hear all, feel all, and can correct all. But in the perfection lies also the danger to the regime. And Domenach adds, here in my translation from the Danish[8]:

> At a close reading of the history of the Gulags of China, it is possible to understand the paradoxes of totalitarian control. This attempt to control the population is at the same time ambitious and dangerous. To be successful in this close control of groups and individuals, the will to rule must be complete and permanent. The history of the Gulags is a history of the consequences when this will withers away … In such a situation, the close control evaporates. The small groups that earlier functioned as instruments of control become isolated. Gradually they develop an experience of joint destiny and shared interest … The system of close control is turned against those who invented the system. This is the reason that the close to perfect Chinese system seems to go to pieces even faster than other systems of similar type.

Up to this point, we have by and large concentrated our attention on Europe, West and East, with some additional excursions to mainland

China. The major impression so far is of a rather unstable situation. The archetypes of welfare states have been able to keep up the standards of a relatively low prison population. But they are under heavy pressure. The two large Gulag-empires have dramatically reduced their number of prisoners, but at least for Russia, that reduction seems not particularly solidly cemented. On the other hand, it is difficult to understand how, in the long run, it will be possible to keep such a large segment of the population in Gulags if these nations admit ideas generally found in Western countries. But again, this is a preliminary conclusion, one drawn before we have embarked on an analysis of the largest industrial power in the world.

Chapter 6

The Trend-Setter

6.1 Whom one loveth, one chasteneth

There are few countries so pleasant to visit as the USA. As a Norwegian, I feel close to home, often better than at home. We often say that there are as many Norwegians in the USA as there are in Norway. They made a good deal by leaving the old country, materially, and maybe also socially. The warm atmosphere in many encounters, the care for new neighbours, the fascination of the variations within the large cities.

These words are being written in an attempt to counteract some completely wrong interpretations of what now follows. I am intending to do the impossible. I am trying to say that I am fundamentally fond of a country and its people, that I feel close to it, also by national heritage. But at the same time, I will claim that there is something extraordinarily alarming in the social fabric of the USA. And precisely because I feel so close, feel the country as so much of myself, it is increasingly difficult to keep quiet and not express my concern.

Most difficult of all is to meet colleagues from the USA. American criminology rules much of the world, their theories on crime and crime control exert an enormous influence. American criminologists are kind and conscientious people, kind to visitors, conscientious in their standards of scientific activitity. Their standards become our standards and their solutions tend to be copied abroad.

Maybe these are the reasons why I think of Germany, from the 1920s and later. Germany, that country of culture and insight, that country of science, that country of rational thoughts and romantic hearts. Norway has always been more oriented towards England and the USA than towards Continental Europe. Oceans were better for transport than mountain roads. But respect for Germany was high. Their legal writers were held in high esteem, as well as their general policy of law and order. Scholars went there. Authorities in police and prosecution went there. They were the influential model, maybe for a little too long.

Today we go to America.

6.2 The great confinement

When Michel Foucault (1967) wrote his book on Madness and Civilisation, he included a chapter on the "Great Confinement". He had France in mind. He described the efforts to keep the deviant classes and categories under control. Hospitals were built, old leprosy-institutions were converted for the purpose, and Paris became a safe city for the bourgeoisie. Foucault also gives figures for the achievements. At the peak, one per cent of the population was institutionalized. And Foucault gives reasons for this great confinement:

> Before having the medical meaning we give it, or that at least we like to suppose it has, confinement was required by something quite different from any concern with curing the sick. What made it necessary was an imperative of labor ... From the beginning, the institution set itself the task of preventing "mendicancy and idleness as the source of all disorders." In fact, this was the last of the great measures that had been taken since the Renaissance to put an end to unemployment or at least to begging (pp. 46–47).

As we have already demonstrated in Section *3.4* on *Global Trends,* the prison population for the whole of the USA will soon be half-way towards Foucault's core example of the great confinement. And the US figures apply to the country as a whole, including states and districts with low figures, while Foucault's figures are for Paris alone and therefore much too large for France as a whole. And the US figures include no mental institutions.

The figures are also showing an explosive growth.

In June 1983, *Correctional Magazine* had this to say about the growth in the prison population of the USA:

> "Fantastic … enormous … terrifying," were the words chosen by Norval Morris of the University of Chicago Law School to describe last year's increase in the U.S. prison population.
>
> "It's an astonishing increase," says Alfred Blumstein of Carnegie-Mellon University in Pittsburgh.
>
> "I am genuinely surprised; that's stunning growth," says Franklin Zimring, director of the Center for Studies in Criminal Justice at the University of Chicago.
>
> "It's even worse than what I had expected," says Kenneth Carlson of Abt Associates in Cambridge, Mass. "It becomes more and more frightening."

This is what these experts said about the growth in the prison population up until 1983. I was also frightened, and put the article aside to write about it. But the figures and the comments were soon to be outdated. Since 1983, in less than ten years, the figures for the number of prisoners have almost doubled.

A more detailed picture of formal control in the USA is presented in *Table 6.2-1*. It shows, first, figures for the three major types of prisons in the USA; Federal prisons, State prisons, and Jails. Federal and State institutions are where the more severe sentences are served. As we can see from the table, the bulk of the prisoners are in Federal and State institutions, while roughly one third of the inmates serve in Jail. But this does not necessarily mean that they only serve short sentences. Due to lack of space in Federal and State prisons, the Jails have been forced to receive prisoners that formally belong to the Federal and State systems. Further down, the Table includes figures for the population on probation and parole.

Table 6.2-1. Population under formal control, USA 1990/1991[*]

			Cumulative
Federal prisons	1991	71 608	71 608
State prisons	1991	751 806	823 414
Jails	1991	429 305	1 252 719
Total prison population 1–3		1 252 719	
Per 100 000 of population			504
On probation	1990	2 670 234	3 922 953
On parole	1990	531 407	4 454 360
Total population under control of penal law:			4 454 360
Per 100 000 of population			1 794

[*] Bureau of Justice Statistics, Prisoners in 1991 (NCJ-134729). Jail figures are estimates. Probation and Parole figures are from 1990.

The general impression given by the Table is the hugeness of the figures. With a total prison population of more than 1.2 million inmates, the USA is now up to 504 per l00,000 inhabitants in prisons and jails. If we then add probation and parole, we find more than 4.5 million under some sort of legal control. 4.5 million, that means 1,794 per l00,000 inhabitants.

To get an impression of the growth leading up to these figures, we can use the period from l989 to l990 where the increase was 8.6 per cent. That meant 58,808 new prisoners in State and Federal institutions. According to Bureau Director Steven B. Dillingham (*Corrections Digest* May l99l, p. 1), this equals a need for about l,l00 new prison beds – that is what they use as their counting unit in the USA – every week. The increase in jails was 5.5 per cent, or 21,230 prisoners, which probably meant that the need for new prison "beds" increased to 1,400 or 1,500 each week.

In this perspective, the great confinement of Foucault's ancient Paris is not so great any more. More than 1.2 million prisoners. It is such a large number that it is difficult to grasp. It is more than the population of Prague, and also more than the total population of Copenhagen. If we also include all those on probation or parole in the USA, we exceed the total population of Norway.

Diagram 6.2-2. Prisoners in USA from 1850 to 1990 per 100.000.

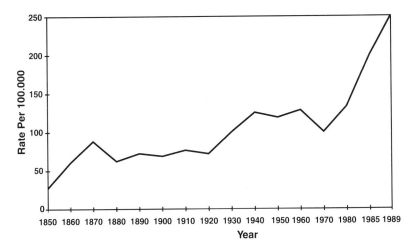

It could, of course, be argued that probation and parole are just formalities without content, or only relatively mild forms of control.
This may be true in some areas, but not everywhere, as documented
in the next chapter.

Also seen in a larger historical perspective, the increase in the prison
population has been quite extraordinary. *Diagram 6.2-2* (from Austin
and McVey 1989, p. 2) shows the development from 1850 to 1989. As
we see from the diagram, the US development is characterized by
three big increases: first from 1850 to 1870, then from 1920 to 1940,
and lastly from 1970 until recently. In the first two periods, the increase came to a stop after twenty years, but this time the growth just
continues. Austin and McVey have also made a five year projection
of the prison population. They expect an increase of 65 per cent up to
1994. That seems to be an under-estimate (conversation with James
Austin).

Those who have arrived in Federal or State institutions will mostly
stay for a very long time. The average stay for those released in 1990
was close to 24 months. But not all are released. 11,759 inmates were
serving what the Americans call "natural life sentences". It is difficult
to see what is natural in their conditions. Behind the formulation is a

Diagram 6.3-1. Prison figures per 100,000 inhabitants 1991 in US, sentenced to more than 1 year in Federal and State Institutions[1]

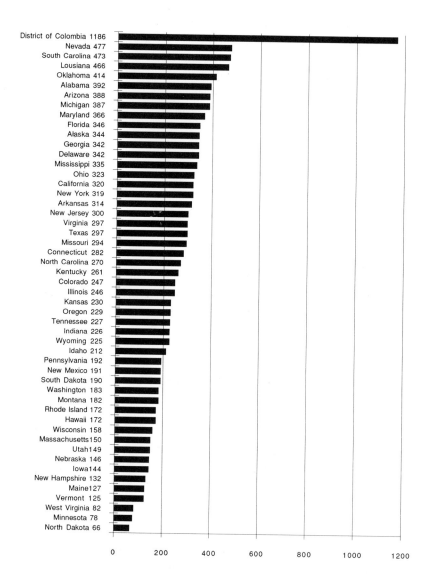

1) Source: Bureau of Justice Statistics: Prisoners in 1991.

decision to keep them in prison for ever. In addition there were 44,451 serving "ordinary" and life sentences. 105,881 were serving sentences of 20 years or more. 2,424 were waiting for execution (*The Corrections Year-book*, 1991). The living conditions for those waiting for execution have been described by Stimson (1991). He ought to know. He is "senior associate in an architectural/engineering/planning firm specializing in quality designed environments for criminal justice facilities". In an article entitled "A Better Design for Safer Detention on Death Row", he describes a design for death row where inmates will have no visual contact with one another, and where they will not be able to communicate. The only people with whom inmates will have contact will be the correctional officers walking the floor. These officers will become familiar with each inmate's behaviour patterns, says Mr. Stimson, and they "will be able to detect anything out of the ordinary" – whatever that might be.

6.3 From state to state

But these United States are not very similar to each other when it comes to punishment. This can be seen from *Table and Diagram 6.3-1.* The major impression is one of extreme variation between the states. While North Dakota, Minnesota and West Virginia are at the very bottom with figures well below one hundred per 100,000 inhabitants, Idaho is over 200, New York is over 300 per 100,000, Oklahoma exceeds the 400 figure, Nevada is close to the 500 level, and the Capital itself, the District of Columbia, leads the nation with the unbelievable figure of 1,168 prisoners sentenced to one year or more per 100,000 resident population. This figure is probably unfair to the capital. Since it is a small geographical area, many come to Washington from districts in the vicinity, are arrested and sentenced there, and count in their statistics.

But evaluating these variations, we have to keep in mind that in all these figures we have only included the more severe sentences of more than one year, and also only those served in Federal and State prisons. This means that more than 460,000 prisoners, or 37 percent, are left out of the Table. North Dakota has 68 prisoners per 100,000 inhabitants in the table. If we estimate the omission also here to be about 37 percent – probably a rather dubious procedure – North Dakota would reach 93 prisoners per l00,000. This means that North Dakota keeps within the West European level of incarceration. But Minnesota and West Virginia already exceed the level of England and Wales with 108 and 112 respectively if we add the 37 per cent, and from then on, all contact with West European standards is gone. Lousiana, Nevada and South Carolina would with such an estimate each end up with more than 600 prisoners per l00,000 inhabitants. Since females are so rare in prison, this means that at least one percent of the male population in these states is in prison at any time.

6.4 States of prisons

Of all the beautiful states, California is probably number one. Here is sun, here is leisure, here is Berkeley and Stanford and the heaven of academic life, here is business and expansion and work, here is the dream-factory of the world: Hollywood.

And here are also some of the more famous prisons in the United States. Alcatraz is gone, but San Quentin remains with a fame stretching far beyond the USA. And here is Folsom with 7,000 prisoners, 500 among them probably never to be released. And in these years, new structures are being added to the great Californian tradition.

California has 101,808 prisoners in Federal and State institutions. Based on those sentenced for one year or more, they have 320 for every l00,000 inhabitants. If we add an estimated 37 per cent for short-termers and those in jails, we end up with 438 prisoners per l00,000 for 1991. But California favours growth and vivacity, and plans for 800 per l00,000 at the turn of the century. And they do not stop at planning, they build. One of the prisons under construction was described like this in *Los Angeles Times* on May 1, 1990:

> Pelican Bay is entirely automated and designed so that inmates have virtually no face-to-face contact with guards or other inmates. For 22 1/2 hours a day, inmates are confined to their windowless cells, built of solid blocks of concrete and stainless steel so that they won't have access to materials they could fashion into weapons. They don't

work in prison industries; they don't have access to recreation; they don't mingle with other inmates. They aren't even allowed to smoke because matches are considered a security risk.

Inmates eat all meals in their cells and leave only for brief showers and 90 minutes of daily exercise. They shower alone and exercise alone in miniature yards of barren patches of cement enclosed by 20 feet high cement walls covered with metal screens. The doors to their cells are opened and closed electronically by a guard in a control booth.

...

There are virtually no bars in the facility; the cell doors are made of perforated sheets of stainless steel with slots for food trays. Nor are there guards with keys on their belts walking the tiers. Instead, the guards are locked away in glass-enclosed control booths and communicate with prisoners through a speaker system.

... The SHU (Secure Housing Unit) has its own infirmary; its own law library (where prisoners are kept in secure rooms and slipped law books through slots); and its own room for parole hearings. Inmates can spend years without stepping outside the Unit.

California's Governor George Deukmejian dedicated the new prison on June 14, 1990. According to *Corrections Digest* (June 27, 1990 p. 9) he stated:

"California now possesses a state-of-the-art prison that will serve as a model for the rest of the nation. ... Pelican Bay symbolises our philosophy that the best way to reduce crime is to put convicted criminals behind bars." The Governor also noted that the annual cost of keeping a convicted felon in prison is $ 20,000 compared with the $ 430,000 that it costs society when a career criminal is at work on the street.

But California is not alone. The *Sunday Oklahoma* of February 24, 1991 has this to report from that state:

Inmates housed in the "high-max" security unit will live 23 hours a day in their cells, with the other hour spent in a small concrete recreation area with 20-foot walls. The space is topped by a metal grate. Theoretically, an inmate could move into the new cellhouse and never again set foot outdoors. The unit's first residents will be the 114 men on death row. The cellhouse also contains a new execution chamber.

The organization Human Rights Watch has investigated prison conditions in the USA. This study is a parallel study to the one by Helsinki Watch on prison conditions in the Soviet Union. In a detailed report

(1992) Human Rights Watch describes trends towards total isolation in the U.S. prisons. They call the trend "Marionization". A federal prison with that name implemented a series of extraordinary security measures in 1983, and 36 states have followed suit in creating their own super maximum security institutions called "Maxi-Maxi" in prison jargon.

> The confinement in "maxi-maxis" is administered by prison officials without independent supervision and leads to a situation in which inmates may in fact be sentenced twice: once by the court, to a certain period of imprisonment; and the second time by the prison administration, to particularly harsh conditions.

> The conditions at Marion are much harsher than in any other federal prison, including confinement of inmates for up to 23 hours a day to their cells and denial of any contact visits (p. 4).

State prisons have the same arrangements. From Florida, this is reported:

> A particularly glaring example is the windowless Q-Wing of the Florida State Prison at Starke, from which inmates never go outside and where some prisoners have been held as long as seven years (p. 4).
> …
> Such a placement is open-ended, and may last, we were informed, for as long as 15 years. The inmate is allowed three showers and two hours of outdoor exercise a week as the only time outside the cell. He can buy a limited number of goods from the canteen and check out one book a week from the library (if he is not on the Library Suspension List, another disciplinary measure at Starke). Inmates under close management can also be deprived of all exercise outside the cell and not allowed outdoors for years at a time. The Florida rules claim that "Close Management is not disciplinary in nature and inmates in close management are not being punished"(p. 44).

Disciplinary confinement is even more serious, meant for prisoners who commit an infraction within the prison. In addition to the restrictions associated with close management, these inmates are not allowed any reading material except legal materials. But life can turn even worse. This prison has a Q-Wing for those who commit further infractions while already in one of the categories described above. Cells here are 6 feet 11 inches by 8 feet 7 inches, with a cement bunk, a toilet and a sink. There is no window and no furniture. The door is of metal. The heat in the cell was stifling, according to the Human Rights Watch (p. 45).

But the US is a land of contrast. The extreme isolation is the one type of evil. But the extreme contrast to isolation also has its costs. The Human Rights Watch also describes these conditions (pp. 19 and 20):

> Jails are supposed to hold inmates for briefer periods than prisons, and that fact is reflected in the physical structure of most institutions. They often have very limited recreation facilities, house inmates in window-less cells, and provide little or no privacy to the detainees.

> For example, the Criminal Justice Centre in Nashville, Tennessee was built in 1982 with a capacity for about 300 inmates. At the time of our visit in 1990, it held more than 800 inmates and we were told that at some point recently it had held 1,100. For over six months, a staff member told us, the facility's gym was used to house several hundred pretrial detainees. They had two bathrooms and two showers at the gym. At the time of the greatest overcrowding, additional space in the underground tunnel leading to the courthouse was used to house 200 inmates. There were no showers and no bathrooms in that area.

> … on Rikers Island in New York City, out of 1,516 inmates at the time of our visit about 300 were housed in cells (mostly segregation) while the rest lived in dormitories and on the decks of converted ferry boats anchored to the shore of the island. Each dormitory housed up to 57 inmates …

> In the Sybil Brand jail in Los Angeles, women slept in dormitories holding between 130-156 people. The dorms were crowded and offered no personal privacy.

The complaints from these prisoners were strikingly similar to those we have quoted earlier from Russians prisoners *(Chapter 5.6):*

> Dormitories were designed for 50, yet held about 90 inmates at the time of our visit. Inmates complained to us about the crowded conditions and about not being able to choose a roommate. A severely overweight woman (she told us her weight was 280 pounds) said that when she and her roommate were both in the cubicle, they literally could not move (p. 34).

> One inmate … described his cell (in another prison): "Peeling paint on walls, leaking plumbing, broken glass in windows, dim lighting,

roaches, rats/mice, ants, mosquitoes, moldy pillows and mattress, covered with filth, which have no plastic covers, unbearable heat in the summer, intense cold in winter."

But the USA is also in other ways a country of contrasts. Again, according to the Human Rights Watch (p. 61):

Among institutions visited by Human Rights Watch, only the Bedford Hills facility allowed inmates who gave birth during incarceration to keep their babies in prison. Under a New York state law, female inmates are allowed to keep their babies for one year.

In addition to accommodations for babies, Bedford Hills, a facility where 75 percent of the inmates are mothers, has arrangements to help them maintain contacts with older children. In the summer, the facility runs week long programs for inmates' children who are housed with local families and spend the day with their mothers on the premises. They play with their mothers in a large, toy-filled visiting room, and may also participate in a number of organized activities. In addition, they can also use a playground outside. Year-round, according to the warden, there are bus rides once a month from New York City and Albany, arranged so that children can visit their mothers without having to be accompanied by other relatives.

6.5 The crime explanation

The conventional explanation of growth in prison rates is to see it as a reflection of growth in crime. The criminal starts it all, and society has to react. This is the re-active thinking. As we already commented in Chapter 3.5, this thinking did not hold up for Europe. And it fares no better in the USA:

The prison population has doubled during the last ten years. But here is what the Bureau of Justice Statistics says (*National Update January 1992,* p. 5) about the number of victims in that period:

Victimization rates continue a downward trend that began a decade ago.

There were approximately 34.4 million personal and household crimes in 1990, compared with 41.4 million in 1981.

From 1973 to 1990, the rate of personal crimes (rape, robbery, assault, personal theft) fell by 24.5% and the rate for household crimes (burglary, household theft, motor vehicle theft) fell by 26.1%

Because the NCVS (The National Crime Victimization Survey) counts only crimes for which the victim can be interviewed, homicides are not counted. Their exclusion does not substantially alter the overall estimates.

The number of victims has gone down. Furthermore, and again in sharp contrast to folk-beliefs on crime in the USA, the number of serious offences reported to the police also shows a slight decrease. The FBI statistics on serious offences started at 5.1 million in 1980 and ended at 4.8 million in 1989. But the severity of the sanctions for these crimes has increased. In 1980, 196 offenders were sentenced to prison for every 1,000 arrests for serious crimes. In 1990 the number of imprisonments for such crimes had increased to 332, according to the Bureau of Justice Statistics on Prisoners in 1990.

Mauer (1991, p. 7) has these comments:

While there is little question that the United States has a high rate of crime, there is much evidence that the increase in the number of people behind bars in recent years is a consequence of harsher criminal justice policies of the past decade, rather than a direct consequence of rising crime.

Austin and Irwin (1990, p. 1) say:

National statistics show that the majority (65 per cent) of offenders are sentenced to prison for property, drug and public disorder crimes. A significant number (15 per cent) of all admissions have not been convicted of any crime but are returned to prison for violating their parole "conditions" (e.g. curfew violations, failure to participate in a program, evidence of drug use, etc.).

From their own research – a study based on a random intake to prisons in three states – they also conclude that the vast majority of inmates are sentenced for petty crimes that involve little danger to public safety, or significant economic loss to victims.

The explosion in the number of prisoners in the USA cannot be explained as "Caused by crime". We have to look for other explanations. They follow in the next chapters.

Chapter 7

Crime control as a product

7.1 The crime control market

From the folklore, we know that everything is bigger in the USA than everywhere else. Nonetheless, to a foreigner it is a moving experience to get in one's hand the official publication of the American Correctional Association. The title is *Corrections Today,* a magazine with glossy pages, in colour and perfect print, containing a quantity of advertisements which is probably a considerable source of income to the Association.

In the issue for June 1991, there were 111 advertisements. Three major categories were represented:

1. Building of prisons, entire prisons, or parts of prisons. There were sixteen such ads. You phone and we build. Six months after your call, the prison is ready. Besteel is one of those. In a full page ad we are told :

> Albany County Jail and Penitentiary. 64 bed dormitory style Jail ... Completed in 6 months.

Bell Construction also has a full page under the title:

> The Pros on Cons.

> For more than 20 years we've been building. Building a reputation. Building a client list, and building correctional facilities. That's all we

do, we build. And we do it well. Twenty-five correctional facilities worth §300 millions have given us the experience, and now our clients call us the "pros".

Are you building or renovating a correctional facility? Are you interested in a design-built facility at a guaranteed price? If you're interested in finding out more about our experience, call Don Estes, senior vice president at ...

Some authorities may be in need of a site for their prisons. The Bibby Line group has a solution according to the ancient tradition of the ship of fools:

Maritime Correctional Facilities.

Times change ... Bibby OFFERS alternatives to land based facilities. Bibby DELIVERS:
– Crisis relief within 90–120 days

– Up to 650 beds within 9–12 months.

2. Equipment for prisons. In this area, the June issue contained 43 ads of all sorts. Among them were three for telephones particularly suitable for prisons, twenty for electronic surveillance systems of all sorts, three for weapons and seven for other security equipment.

Phones that enforce

is a whole page ad by USWEST Communication:

This phone only does what *you* want it to do. It controls how long callers talk. It bars them from reaching certain numbers. It can monitor and record all phone activity, as directed...Keep inmate telephone privileges firmly under your control ...

Or:

Designed for Criminal Justice Professionals: Drug Abuse? Yes or no in 3 minutes ... Rapid results leave no time for alibis. ... ONTRAK allows no time for excuses and gives you complete control of the testing situation.

"PRISON BAND"

Identify inmates with a heavy duty waterproof wristband. Two locking metal snaps insure a non-transferable heavy duty no-stretch identification system. No special tools are needed to close our metal snaps. Both write on surface and insert card systems are available. SECUR-BAND, the answer for inmate indentification.

The issue of *Corrections Today* for June carried an enormous number of advertisements, but that issue was soon to be dwarfed. In July the number of pages increased from 160 to 256. Ordinary ads increased from 111 to 130. Partly they were of the same types as in June, like the one for tear gas:

The TG Guard system, now installed in major prisons, is a strategic arrangement of tear gas dispensers installed at the ceiling level. These dispensers can be fired from a remote-control console by protected personnel. The firing can be in a chosen pattern and with various levels of concentration to force the inmates to evacuate an area in a route which you determine.

If tear gas is not sufficient, Point Blank Body Armour is available:

Some inmates would *love* to stab, slash, pound, punch and burn you. But they won't get past your S.T.A.R. Special Tactical Anti-Riot vest.

In addition to the usual ads, the July issue also contained sixty yellow pages called:

Buyer's Guide of Correctional Products and Services.

Here were listed 269 companies, with a specification of their products, from A – Access Control system, via P- Portable Jail Cells, down to X for X-ray and security screening equipment. The list shows the latest in electronics, but also firms with traditions, like the:

Human Restraint Company

Finest quality leather restraints. Manufactured in USA since 1876. Call or write for a free brochure.

This official publication of the American Correctional Association does not only contain paid advertisements. It also carries articles, squeezed in between the ads. But several of the articles are written by employees of the very same firms which advertise in the journal. The July issue has an article by Ostroski and Rohn, both from Precision Dynamics Corporation, a manufacturer of identification systems. Here is what they tell us from Los Angeles, which has, in their own words, the largest single detention facility "in the free world". In this extraordinary place they have trusted inmate identification wristbands for almost 14 years. But Georgia has a more sophisticated system:

> the crowded DeKalb County Jail near Atlanta, Ga., houses more than 1,200 inmates. In the winter of 1989, officials there decided to begin using bar code wristbands that employ the same basic technology as bar codes used in clothing stores and supermarkets.
> …
> To create a rehabilitative atmosphere – and still maintain a high security level – jail officials installed a laser-scanning and portable data-collection system to identify and monitor the inmates.
>
> By using hand-held laser units to scan the wristbands, deputies enter data into a small computer.This method of gathering information eliminates the paperwork involved in monitoring inmate movements.
> …
> Technology is now being developed to allow inmate photos to appear on the same wristband as the bar-coded informations. …Inmates can't switch bands, which prevents erroneous releases (pp. 142–145).

Two pictures illustrate the article. Both show black arms – nothing more – with wristbands controlled by white arms in one picture, and by the whole of a white person in the second picture. It is probably not possible to get much closer than that to humans being handled as commodities, based on a technology so well known from the supermarkets.

3. The running of prisons also plays a prominent part, with twenty ads in the June issue:

> When morale's on the line with every meal, count on us. … Service America is working behind bars all across the country, with a solid record of good behavior … If feeding a captive audience is part of your

job, talk to the food service specialists who know how to do justice. Call..

Another condition for peace is efficient weapons. Efficient firms provide non-lethal as well as lethal weapons. Among the non-lethal:

Cap-Stun II
Used by the FBI and 1100 Law Enforcement agencies
Never a law suit involving Cap-Stun in 14 years of use
Proven effective against Drug Abusers and Psychotics
Consumer models available for friends and loved ones

Among the 111 advertisements in June, there were also a few for ordinary products for ordinary people, not particularly relevant to the prison markets.

The July issue also contains two other extraordinary items. The one consists of several pages of thanks to the sponsors of the banquet to be held at the 121st Congress of Correction in Minneapolis, August 1991. From telephone-companies to manufacturers of bullet-proof glass, they pay, and the prison officers celebrate. An additional attractive feature of the stay in Minneapolis is that you can leave that town "in a beautiful, sporty, brand-spanking-new 1991 Dodge Daytona ES fully equipped with every imaginable accessory!" The only condition is that you visit the Exhibit Hall where the industry shows its products, and leave proof that you have been there. When you are registered in the Hall, you are automatically a participant in the lottery for the car.

*

One personal note, on the adaptability of man: On my first reading of *Corrections Today,* I was close to not trusting my own eyes. The image of the prisoners that emerged through the ads was close to unbelievable. So was the frank exposure of the relationship between the correctional establishment and the industrial interests. Medical journals are of course similar, and pharmaceutical firms excel in their briberies of doctors through sponsorship of their congresses, seminars, trips to Hawaii with spouses included and all that. But doctors are supposed to be of some benefit to their patients. The American Correctional Association is of another kind. It is the organization with the mandate to administer the ultimate power of society. It is an organization for the delivery of pain, here sponsored by those who make the tools.

But then, to continue my personal note; the next shock came some weeks later, when I re-read the journals. Now the ads no longer had quite the same punch. I saw advertisements for gas dispensers in the ceiling of prisons without immediately connecting the picture or the text to old images of extermination camps, and I read without great excitement about inmates who would love to stab, slash, pound, punch and burn me and other readers. I had got accustomed to it, domesticated to a highly peculiar perspective on fellow beings, and I had also acquired new (reduced) minimum standards for what sort of surroundings some people can decide that other people have to live in.

7.2 The money push

It must be obvious by now, so I shall be brief: Prison means money. Big money. Big in building, big in providing equipment. And big in running. This is so, regardless of private or public ownership. In all western systems, private firms are involved in some way or other.

Even the relatively small Federal prison system of the USA comes up with enormous figures. For 1992, the system is requesting more than $ 2.1 billion. This is a 24 per cent increase over last year (*The Washington Post*, April 25 1991). According to Knepper and Lilly (1991):

> As prison populations exploded, punishment became big business. If the prison population continues to grow at the 1980s rate, it will cost at least $ 100 million per week just for construction of new facilities. In 1990, total capital and operational expenditures by county, state and federal correctional systems were estimated to be more than $ 25 billion.

Health care and food service are two of the fastest growing sectors in the booming corrections industry, say Knepper and Lilly. In June, the Campbell Soup Company reported that the nation's prison system was the fastest growing food service market. But the biggest profits are made in construction and finance (p. 5):

> The average cost of a US prison bed in 1991–1992 is $ 53,100, up from $ 42,000 in 1987–1988. Not surprisingly, more than a hundred firms specialize in prison architecture alone, and these firms now receive between $ 4 billion and $ 6 billion in prison construction business a year.

Feeley (1991a, pp. 1–2) describes some of it like this:

> As of October 1988, more than 25 for-profit companies, many backed by venture capital, were competing for rights to build, own, and operate jails and prisons throughout the United States (Private Vendors in Corrections, 1988). Privatization in juvenile correction has grown at an even faster pace. During the past thirty years, placements in private programs (e.g. training centers, residential treatment and counselling programs, foster care, and diversion programs) in lieu of state-run facilities have become quite common, and currently in the United States a substantial portion of all juveniles under court supervision are in the custody of privately operated programs. And in recent years jails, prisons, and juvenile facilities have also turned to private vendors to supply a host of services, including food, health, counselling, vocational training, education....

Furthermore, in recent years the private sector has also radically altered the ways correctional facilities are financed and built. Private lease-purchase arrangements are increasingly replacing government-issued bonds.

Private money is into it all. But the most clear-cut case can of course be found in the private prison itself. Let us turn to that.

7.3 Private prisons

> Even capital punishment is sometimes administered by private contractors in the United States today.

I find the sentence in a major book on private prisons (Logan 1990, p. 59). There is just this one sentence on capital punishment, squeezed in between examples of all other tasks administered by private agents. So, for the rest we are free to use our imaginations. And I wonder: private contractors for capital punishment – who are they in modern times, and how do they operate? Do they advertise their service? Is it a private, personally-owned firm, or is it registered on the stock exchange as Pain-Delivery Ltd. Limited liability – limited to what? And what about the equipment needed, chairs, needles, the poison? Do they provide it themselves, or sub-contract? And the training of the staff – do they use the available know-how? Joseph Ingle (personal communication, but see also his book of 1990) has described the phenomenon of the left-leg man – he who, in a team of six, specializes in fastening the strap around the left leg, this in contrast to the right-legger. Six specialists, reducing the man to die to six parts of a thing.

Why react like this to killing by private contractors? Those to be executed are certainly sentenced by ordinary courts. It all follows basic rules, and officials of the state will certainly see to it that everything is done as decided by that state. The whole execution may actually be better performed than if the state had fumbled with it. The last meal may be better prepared, the psychiatrists and priest may be top performers in their professions, far beyond the reach of ordinary state budgets, and the killing itself may take place without the embarrassing aborted attempts sometimes reported from the state service. Those to be killed would probably appreciate the private quality.

This is the basic line of reasoning in the book by Logan, the only difference being that he writes about the private prison, not the private execution. His conclusion regarding private prisons is clear. All the state is doing, private enterprise can do better, or equally well:

> Arguments against private prisons vary in soundness and plausibility, but in no area have I found any potential problem with private prisons that is not at least matched by an identical or a closely corresponding problem among prisons that are run by the government. … Because they raise no problems that are both unique and insurmountable, private prisons should be allowed to compete (and cooperate) with government agencies so that we can discover how best to run prisons that are safe, secure, humane, efficient, and just (p. 5).

I remain unconvinced, and slightly upset. Why is it that what is so clear to Logan is so utterly unclear to me? His well-ordered book contains a whole chapter on the propriety of private prisons (pp. 49–75). And he finds it proper:

> Our elected leaders exercise very little direct power; rather, they issue instructions and directives that are carried out by subordinates ... However, it is false to assume that the integrity of a chain of civil servants is necessarily superior to a contractual chain.

Behind this reasoning is John Locke, and particularly Robert Nozick in his earlier writings (e.g.1974). They lead Logan to this statement (p. 52):

> In the classical liberal (or in modern terms, libertarian) tradition on which the American system of government is founded, all rights are individual, not collective. The state is artificial and has no authority, legitimate power, or rights of its own other than those transferred to it by individuals.

With this perspective, I can understand Logan's private killing and wish for the privatization of pain delivery in general. But it is at the same time an arrangement which can easily develop into a monster, a monster with a soft surface. Robert P. Weiss (1989, p. 38) describes that surface:

> private prison companies ... have dispensed with paramilitary uniforms and ranking; martial vocabulary and regiment, which have characterized the penal profession since the inception of the penitentiary, are no longer employed. Prison companies still want to create the illusion of legitimate authority, but a business-like image is projected instead of a pseudo-official one. At CCA-run facilities, for example, prisoners are not referred to as 'inmates', instead they are called 'residents', and guards are referred to as 'resident supervisors'. Dressed in camel-coloured sweaters that bear a discreet company insignia, private guards are represented as what one might call 'corporate security technicians'.

Logan's state is a contractual state. Private persons elect a representative. The representative hires a firm to deliver punishments. If the firm is bad, a new one is hired. The private guard represents his firm. There is nothing more to represent, the state is an artifact. But this means that the guard is under diminished control.

In the opposite case, where the state exists, the prison officer is my man. I would hold a hand on his key, or on the switch for the electric chair. He could be a bad officer. And I could be bad. Together we made for a bad system, so well known from the history of punishments. But I would have known I was a responsible part of the arrangement. Chances would also be great that some people in the system were not only bad. They would more easily be personally mobilized. The guard was their guard, their responsibility, not an employee of a branch of General Motors, or Volvo for that matter. The communal character of punishments evaporates in the proposals for private prisons. Since the modern private prison is so much an American invention, it is tempting to ask if they have forgotten their old teacher Charles Horton Cooley (1864–1929) who so clearly saw community as the bed of individuality.

Far back in time, we used to mock – fondly – civil servants as persons with two pots of ink on their desks, one for official and the other for private letters. Those days are gone, but not completely. This can be seen if civil servants are found guilty of some kinds of offences, presenting bills for the same air-travel twice, or whatever. Such abuses are mostly seen as more serious matters than if ordinary, private persons commit them. The civil servant represents more than himself, she or he represents the community, that is me. The servant of the state is thus under greater responsibility and control than those who only serve the private firm. This brings us back to the question of honour. If I live under "communal conditions", politicians are a part of me. But so are those given the task and symbolic quality of being state servants with the mandate to carry out essential functions. Their failure is my shame, their success and decency my pride.

Perhaps this view is more foreign to a reader in the USA where private interests and the contractual state have a stronger hold, than to a European, where the state has existed, forever. Dahrendorf (1985) describes those unbelievable days of Berlin in 1945, the interval between two regimes, when the nazi-state collapsed and the USSR took over. Some days without state power, and then back to normal conditions where a state, just a different one, was in command. Perhaps Flemming Balvig (in comments to my manuscript) is right when he says that Europeans to a larger extent regard both national states and national cultures as something that has always existed, something given, while this for Americans, to a somewhat larger extent, is something created by them as individuals. Logan's contractual states may be in harmony with the American self-understanding. But these differences are far from clear-cut. Jessica Mitford ends her book like this (1974, p. 297):

> Those of us on the outside do not like to think of wardens and guards as our surrogates. Yet they are, and they are intimately locked in a deadly embrace with their human captives behind the prison walls. By extension so are we.
>
> A terrible double meaning is thus imparted to the original question of human ethics: Am I my brother's keeper?

Maybe respect for the civil servant is on the decline on both sides of the Atlantic. Historically, the civil servant was the King's man, civil only in contrast to a military servant. With reduced Royal power, he became – in theory – the servant of the state. In that capacity, this servant has a potentiality for tuning in to the whole set of values in a particular society, values expressed by politicians, by the public in general, or by all sorts of experts. But with the immense growth in the state-administrations of modern nations, another danger becomes imminent: civil servants may end up as servants to their own group, to civil servants in general. The history of the apparatchiks in the former USSR is the prime example of such a development.

7.4 Private police

A similar line of reasoning as the one on private prisons can be formulated regarding private police. This is what Rosenthal and Hoogenboom do in a report to the Council of Europe (1990, p. 39):

> Imagine that private policemen were to handle matters more efficiently and more effectively than governmental police forces. Imagine, to take it a step further, that private policemen were also to treat people equally and according to each and every standard of equity. Then, in spite of the satisfactory fulfillment of all those extrinsic conditions, this would not be sufficient evidence in favour of private policing. In a continental setting, people may feel better about the state doing the job – irrespective of the relative quality of its performance.

But developments in most industrialized nations reveal no sensitivity to this problem. On the contrary, there is a definite trend towards a large expansion in the sector of private policing. The types of private prisons discussed above are still of minor importance compared to the public ones. Even in the USA, their share of the punishment market probably does not exceed some 10–12 per cent. But private security is expanding, both in the USA and in Europe. In a report from the National Institute of Justice in Washington, Cunningham et al. (1991, pp. 1–5) state:

> Private security is now clearly the Nation's primary protective resource, outspending public law enforcement by 73 percent and employing 2 1/2 times the workforce, according to a new National Institute of Justice (NIJ) study of the private security industry. Currently, annual spending for private security is $ 52 billion, and private security agencies employ 1.5 million persons. Public law enforcement spends $ 30 billion a year and has a workforce of approximately 600,000.

Nine categories are identified as part of the private security industry:

> Proprietary (in-house) security.
> Guard and patrol services.
> Alarm services.
> Private investigations.
> Armoured car services.
> Manufacturers of security equipment.
> Locksmiths.
> Security consultants and engineers.
> "Other", which includes categories such as guard dogs, drug testing, forensic analysis, and honesty testing.

Diagrams 7.4-1 and *7.4-2* are both taken from the report. The first shows the number of persons estimated to work for private security compared to those working for the public one. The second shows spending in billions of dollars. The "Crossover point" at 1977 means that 1977 was the year where more money was used on private than on public security. And in the words of the authors:

> While public expenditures for law enforcement will reach $44 billion by the year 2000, they will be dwarfed by private security expenditures, which will reach $104 billion. The average annual rate of growth in private security will be 8 percent, or double that of public law enforcement.

Diagram 7.4-1. Private Security and Law Enforcement Employment

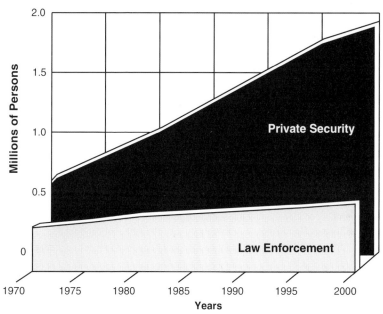

Diagram 7.4-2. Private Security and Law Enforcement Spending

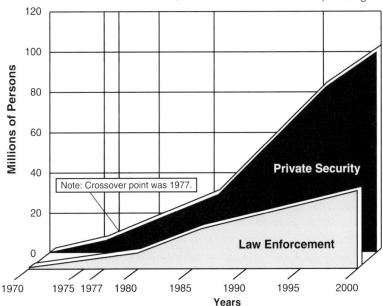

This growth does not take place in splendid isolation from the ordinary police. Earlier, there were few collaborative efforts between police and private security groups, but this has changed:

> In the 1980's however, the International Association of Chiefs of Police, the National Sheriffs' Association, and the American Society for Industrial Security began joint meetings to foster better cooperation between the public and private sectors. In 1986, with funding from the National Institute of Justice, these organizations set up the Joint Council of Law Enforcement and Private Security Associations. A number of local and regional groups also set up cooperative programs involving the police and private security.

Great Britain shows the same development. And it has come to stay. South (1989, p. 97) writes:

> in foreseeable future circumstances it is unlikely, to say the least, that the private security sector is going to go away. It has been a buoyant and 'recession resistant' industry in most major Western economies since, at least, the 1960s, and all indications suggest that it will continue to grow.

France is in the same situation. Ocqueteau (1990, p. 57) describes how private operators have overtaken or are overtaking state bodies in the United States and Canada.

> ... that is not yet the case for the European mainland. And yet it has been estimated that in France, the country thought to have the highest police complement per inhabitant in Europe, there are three private operators for every five members of the state police force.

This development raises severe problems. But the similarity to the prison arena is not total, as revealed in the stimulating writings of Shearing and Stenning (e.g.1987), and also in an important article by Phillipe Robert (1989). They begin by considering three major points. First, police have of course evolved from being private to becoming the public instrument for the state. Thus, private police is nothing new. Second, with the development of materially rich, large-scale societies, the ordinary police have no chance whatsoever of clearing up more than a tiny fragment of all problems brought before them. This will increase the pressure for alternative solutions. And here comes their third point: Private police are, under normal circumstances, also forced to behave as private persons or organizations tend to do. They do not have the penal apparatus at their disposal. They are therefore not particularly oriented towards punishment:

> ... the logic of private security systems is blatantly managerial, concerned with risk management, reducing investment at the least possible cost. Repression is far from being a priority: it is counterproductive to the firm's aims, as well as expensive, since it usually involves the use of public agencies. Prevention, rationalization and compromise are therefore given top priority (Robert, p. 111).

This, again, opens for possibilities of more civil solutions to conflict where otherwise penal law would be seen as the only – and badly – functioning alternative.

Private police are dependent on having the public police available – as a last resort. But it decreases the authority of the private agency to have to turn to the public one. And it is a dangerous strategy. The efficiency of the private one is dependent on a belief in the public that the ordinary police would give the private agency full support if asked to. Maybe they would not.

While private prisons increase the capacity for incarceration, private police might lead to reduced use of imprisonment. In this perspective, recent developments are not that unattractive. In the opinion of Shearing and Stenning, the contemporary private police are evidence of the re-emergence of private authorities who sometimes effectively challenge the state's claimed monopoly over the definition of order (1987, p. 13):

> ... what is now known about private policing provides compelling evidence ... that what we are witnessing through the growth of private policing is not merely a reshuffling of responsibility for policing public order but the emergence of privately defined orders, policed by privately employed agents, that are in some cases inconsistent with, or even in conflict with, the public order proclaimed by the state.

But the possible gain of getting control away from the domain of penal law – the dream-situation for the abolitionist thinkers – has to be balanced against the two major defects of the private police: their class bias and their potentialities for abuse in situations of severe political conflicts.

The class bias has two sides. Least problematic is the obvious fact that upper-class people will be easily able to buy themselves out of embarrassing situations. This is so also within the ordinary penal system. It is close to obvious that all formal systems of control concentrate attention on the strata of the population at a safe distance from the power-holders. Exceptional cases of powerful figures brought before the courts are just that: exceptional. A much more problematic effect of private police is that they leave lower class areas and interests unprotected. This is the central message from The New Realists in Great Britain – with Young and Matthews (1992), Young (1989) and Lea and Young (1984) as some of the major exponents. These are completely right when they say that the labour class, and those below, are particularly menaced by ordinary theft, violence and vandalism. A private police, caring for those able and willing to pay, might reduce the interest among the upper classes in having a good, public police, and thus leave the other classes and the inner cities in an even worse situation.

In addition comes the problem of the control of the controllers. How to prevent the private police from becoming a power even more difficult to control than the recent public police? How to ensure that the public police will not hire, formally or informally, some of the private ones to do what the public police are not supposed to do? How to prevent State power from getting some much wanted help from private groups not hampered by all those soft-handed judges and lawyers?

If the Gestapo or the KGB had been branches of a private firm, hired by dictators, they might have been equally efficient and ugly in their methods, but would not to the same extent have intimidated their state régimes. When parts of the crime control system belong to the state, there is at least some hope that those parts will be destroyed when the state is destroyed. Hope, but no certainty, as recent developments in several East European states indicate. But if they are private, they are even more protected when the régime falls. Then they belong to a type of organization where both trans-national and national interests see to it that they are allowed to continue. The Gestapo and the SS-troops were eleminated after the Second World War, but the firms that provided the equipment for the camps and received the prisoners as slave labourers are very much alive in Germany today. So are the universities that received research material from the camps.

7.5 The private push

The essential features of modernity in crime control are illustrated in the privatization movement, and particularly in the re-invention of the private prison. This type of prison is not – in volume of prisoners – the dominant type anywhere in the industrialized world. But it is on its way in, particularly in the United States, along with spiritual off-spring in several European countries. And it is of importance, since it typifies recent trends.

The private prison does not represent a continuation of the old idea of galley slaves and workhouses. The model is municipal care for the poor. Auctions were often arranged. Those who had the lowest bid got the goods – the care of the poor. Possibilities for profit in running poor houses is a debated topic. But with the large-scale arrangements now growing up, no doubt remains. Here it is a question of big money. And, most importantly, with this amount of interplay with private profit interests, even up to the level of private prisons, we are building an important growth factor into the system.

The general debate on "privatization" of prisons, and also of police, has to a large extent been focused on ethics: should private companies be given the right to apply this amount of force? Or the debate has been on the economy: will private companies be able to run it more cheaply than the state? But equally important is an awareness of the expansive drive created in a system based on privatization. The central question is, as stated by Feeley (1990, p. 2) *to what extent does privatization expand and transform the state's capacity to punish.*

Logan's (1990) view is that privatization will not necessarily lead to increased capacity in prisons:

> On the whole, however, businesses succeed not by stimulating spurious demand, but by accurately anticipating both the nature and the level of real demand (p. 159).

And how then do you decide what the "real demand" is?

> prison flow should respond to the crime rate, which is largely beyond the control of the state; therefore, prison capacity must be flexible (p. 170).

Right now, there is – according to Logan – a genuine unmet demand for imprisonment (p. 161). And this is worse than oversupply:

> If both oversupply and undersupply can lead to injustice, we should, in principle, err on the side of oversupply, although this is not likely to happen for some time to come (pp. 151–152).

He is so right, particularly based on his own data two pages further on:

> Those who said that the courts were not harsh enough rose steadily from 48.9 per cent in 1965 to 84.9 per cent in 1978. ... from 1980 to 1986, between 82 and 86 per cent of Americans advocated stiffer penalties for lawbreakers.

With a view on crime as an unlimited natural resource for the crime control industry, we see the dangers in this type of reasoning. The economic interests of the industry, with confirmation from Logan, will all the time be on the side of oversupply, both of police and of prison capacity. This establishes an extraordinarily strong force for expansion of the system.

In addition comes the fact that privatization makes it simple both to build and to run prisons. Advocates of private prisons are in trouble here. It is difficult both to argue for the speed, flexibility and economic advantages of privately run prisons, and at the same time claim that these advantages will not lead to an oversupply. Logan describes the advantages (p. 79):

> Private companies have demonstrated repeatedly that they can locate, finance, design, and construct prisons more rapidly than the government can. Corrections Corporation of America reports its construction costs to be about 80 per cent of what the government pays for construction. CCA notes that it can build not only faster, thereby saving inflation costs, but also at a lower immediate cost, since construction contractors charge the government more.

Private financing also makes for a simpler life for government, since it does not need to ask the voters for permission to build new prisons. In Logan's words, "... it avoids the cost of a referendum" (p. 79). It also makes it simpler to run the prisons since strikes by employees can more easily be prevented:

> Since a strike or other disruption would allow the government to terminate a contract, unemployment as the result of a strike will be a credible threat to private officers. In contrast, such threats do not often deter strikes in the public sector.

As a help, also to the public sector, Logan suggests:

> to couple legislation requiring that all correctional officers – public and private – be certified, with legislation providing for automatic decertification of officers who participate in a strike.

With private prisons as the extreme example, but also with the economic/industrial establishment as providers of services to prisons run by the public, a highly efficient growth factor is built into the system. Just as illustrated in *Corrections Today:* Interested sellers line up, their tools for the efficient delivery of suffering are displayed, and the prospective buyers are bribed to come and see. When the government is also given help both to avoid their voters and to prevent strikes among the staff, highly efficient mechanisms for expansion are created.

An additional growth factor is the "mental adaptation" created by the many forecasts within the area. As stated in written comments from Flemming Balvig to my manuscript:

> forecasts are a tool of management. It removes the shock in the development. It can not be otherwise. 200,000 prisoners in California in year 2000? This we have known for long. And maybe we end at 190,000 – so, the conditions have not turned out quite as bad as predicted.

Thus the interest becomes focused on the accuracy of the forecasts, not on the horror in the development, not on how to prevent forecasts from coming true.

7.6 The technological push

The extraordinary growth in the prison figures for California from 1980 to 1990 has been close to a mystery. Those years were affluent years in California. Frank Zimring (1991, p. 22) has a diagram for the period showing the rate of unemployment moving dramatically downwards, while the rate of imprisonment ascends straight to heaven. Messinger and Berecochea also has confusing data. They can show that time served in prison up to first release has gone down steadily the last ten to fifteen years. For a while, the median for males was more than 36 months, but in recent years it has dropped to close to 12 months. This should lead to half-empty prisons in California. But it has not, and Messinger and Berecochea has an explanation: Stays in prison are shorter, but stays outside prison are also a sort of prison, at least for those on early release. Prisoners are released on probation. And probation has changed its character. *Diagram 7.6-1.* is from Messinger and Berecochea (1991, p. 43), and shows the development from 1975 to 1987. What is illustrated here is that release from prison is only a temporary release. In the words of the authors:

> ... release, increasingly, is not the end of the story. Until the first quarter of the 20th century, a first-release from prison was for most prisoners almost certainly the last – on their current conviction, at least: prisoners were discharged from sentence at the prison gate. Next, for the majority of prisoners, first-release from prison served as a gateway to a period of parole-supervision. Even then, however, until the relatively recent past, the first-release from prison was the last under the current conviction: most were discharged at the end of the parole period. Currently, this is not the case; return to prison has become not a rarity but the most common experience for prisoners. Sentences of imprisonment are being served on the instalment plan.

And why is that so?

For two reasons. First, probation in California was in danger of losing ground – and jobs. To survive, probation officers had to choose sides, – between being social workers without jobs, or crime-controllers with both jobs and guns. They chose the latter alternative in a move which illustrates so much of what Stan Cohen (1985) has discussed as role-blurring. Smith (1991, p. 114) describes the development:

Diagram 7.6-1. Returns to Prison Within Two Years. By Years of Parole

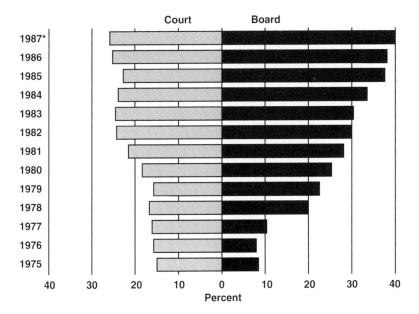

In the late '70 s there was a shift in California parole's role from rehabilitation and service to control and enforcement. This was driven by changes in public attitudes and in the law defining the role of prison and parole to be punitive rather than rehabilitative. Further, there was a serious attempt to statutorily abolish parole. It became clear that if parole was to survive, it would have to take a more aggressive approach.

So, probation officers got their guns. Again according to Smith (p. 124):

We selected the Smith & Wesson Model 64 .38-calibre revolver. It is relatively lightweight, stainless steel, with a two inch barrel. It carries six rounds and is easy to conceal under the clothes agents normally wear. We chose ammunition that had the maximum stopping power without fragmenting.

Florida is doing the same. Their Department of Corrections has announced that probation and parole officers will be authorized to wear firearms beginning July 1 (*Correctional Digest,* January 8, p. 10, 1992).

The other reason for the great increase in return to prisons, is that science and technology came to the assistance of the probation workers. Again according to Messinger, this time in his oral presentation (p. 36):

> something like 400,000 drug tests were done last year on parolees here. I think that's one heck of a lot of urine that has to be taken.

What has happened is that early release is being followed by tight control, and now that the technology is there, it is eagerly used. At intervals, released prisoners are forced to pee. They belong to the segment of the population where drug use is part of the life-style. Before, while probation was still social work, they might have received mild warnings, and hopefully some help to survive. Now a technique exists for control, and back to prison they go. It is a beautiful example of management of the dangerous classes. Now it is not necessarily the original crime which brings them back to prison. It is something in their life-style. Control of drugs means control of the lower classes.

In addition to those returned to prison because of drug use under parole, come those sentenced directly for drug offences. Together these two categories make up a majority of the prison population. In 1986 they were 30 per cent, in 1988 35 per cent, and in 1991 53 per cent of the prison population. In 1995, according to federal prison director Michael J. Quinlan, drug offenders in federal prisons will account for 69 per cent of the prison population (*The Washington Post,* April 1991). Austin (1991) documents much the same development at the state level in Florida. But this trend is also, as documented in *Chapter 5.5,* clearly visible in European welfare states. Everywhere in modern states, drugs become the major form of deviance used as a key to the control of those at the bottom of society. With a little help from the drug-testing industry, these possibilities are close to unlimited.

The only weak link in the system is the lack of prison capacity. But here, too, industry offers a helping hand. The electronically governed home prison has recently taken a giant stride.

The principles in this type of home prison have long been known, and applied. The prisoner gets an electronic device around his wrist or ankle. The bracelet is connected to the telephone. If the home-prisoner leaves the house, the connection to the telephone is broken, and an alarm sounds in the police or probation headquarters. There is a blossoming market for this device, particularaly in the USA, but also abroad. Singapore recently bought equipment worth $ 7 millions in one single transaction (Lacotte 1991).

But the system has one weakness: one cannot know, exactly, what the prisoners do at home. They are, of course, not allowed to touch liquor at home – in their prisons. Maybe they do.

Mitsubishi has solved this problem and brought law and order into American home prisons. In a full-page ad in *Corrections Today* of June 1991, we are shown a whole control package. It contains the usual electronic bracelet, but in addition there is a telephone combined with a television transmitter and a device for testing the blood alcohol level. Soon, I feel sure, televized urinating will also be added. Here is an excerpt of what Mitsubishi describes:

> To meet the growing needs in home detention, a monitoring system must be versatile, reliable, and capable of checking alcohol usage. The risk is too high to settle for less.
> ...
> The system automatically calls the client (up to 4 at a time), requests some action (in any language), and records the picture with time, date, and name (providing hard evidence).
> ...
> When it comes to Breath Alcohol Testing (BAT), only MEMS provides remote, unassisted, positive visual proof of a client's blood alcohol level and his identity. And, it's all done automatically from the computer base station.

7.7 Raw-material for control

Prison, then, solves several problems in highly industrialized countries. It softens the dissonance in welfare states between the idea of care for the unemployed and the idea that the pleasure of consumption should be a result of production. It also brings parts of the idle population under direct control, and creates new tasks for the industry and its owners. In this last perspective, prisoners acquire a new and important role. They become raw material for control. It is an ingenious device. Welfare cheques provided money which could be used for questionable purposes. To prevent that, welfare was sometimes given in goods, or as requisitions to buy specified necessities. But some recipients would still cheat, and exchange the healthy products for drugs or drinks. Prisons solve this problem. The material standards in some modern prisons are incredibly high. But the consumption is under complete control, an ultimate solution to the ancient problem of industrialization. The potentially dangerous population is taken away and placed under complete control as raw material for parts of the very same industrial complex which made them superfluous and idle outside the walls. Raw material for control, or, if you like, captive consumers of the services of the control industry.

It would have been even more ideal if these prisoners combined being raw material for control with efficient production. Then they would have provided both work for the guards, and commodities for society in general. But this combination seems extraordinarily difficult to get going in industrialized societies of the Western type. *Business Weekly* reports that some 5,000 US inmates are working for private industry. 5,000 – out of 1.2 million. Prisoners are important for the economy of the US, but that is for what they need for keep and food, not for what they produce.[1]

7.8 The great American tradition

Penal development in the USA has changed dramatically in the last ten years. But seen in the perspective of centuries, nothing is really new. On the contrary, it was the period after World War II which constituted the exception. Now the United States is actually moving back

---

1 But in China, the article in *Business Weekly* made large headlines. "The national television news and most major newspapers, all run by the communist government, gave prominent coverage to an account about American-style prison labour published in the Feb. 17 issue of Business Week. ...The Chinese reports carried the strong suggestion that the U.S. Government, which accuses China of exporting prisoner-made goods to the United States in violation of U.S. law, should practice what it preaches or change the sermon." *Correctional Digest*, February 19, p.10, 1992.

to normal, only with more strength to do so. Two key terms characterize the situation: Privatization and Slavery.

Privatization is nothing new. It was with privatization it all started, first in England and later in the USA. Prosecution was private, the police were private, local prisons were private – run by alehouse-keepers. Most importantly, transportation was a result of private initiative and business instincts. The result was that some 50,000 convicts were shipped across the Atlantic. In the words of Feeley (1991a, p. 3):

> Shortly after the first colonists arrived in Virginia in 1607, they were followed by a handful of convicted felons transported there as a condition of pardon to be sold into servitude. Thus was set into motion a new penal system, a system that operated successfully for nearly 250 years...
>
> ... transportation to the New World was a marriage of efficiency and effectiveness. Most of its costs were borne by profit-seeking merchants selling their human cargo and by planters who purchased it. It was effective in that it sanctioned thousands of offenders who otherwise would have gone unpunished.
>
> ... transportation was an innovation promoted by mercantile interests which was only reluctantly embraced by public officials as they slowly came to appreciate its cost effectiveness.
>
> ... The policy of transportation multiplied the state's penal capacity and at low cost to the government. It expanded the reach and efficacy of the criminal sanction without the need for a centralized bureaucracy.

And the tradition of privatization was directly converted into prison area. When transportation came to an end, some of the surplus ships were placed in San Francisco Bay. Maritime Correctional Facilities as advertised by the Bibby Line group have a long history. In the San Francisco Bay they housed convicts while they built the prison at San Quentin. The many famous early prisons built in the United States of America were also dependent on money from the private contractors who used convict labour. Several large prisons were leased to private contractors.

> The size of the prison population was determined not by the amount of crime or the need for social control or the efficiency of the police, but by the desire to make crime pay – for government and private employees.

It is Novak (1982) who says this, here quoted by Ericson, McMahon and Evans (1987, p. 358) in an article with the telling title "Punishing for Profit". And they add that

> The Mississippi prison system celebrated the fact that it turned a profit every year until the Second World War. It was only in the late 1920s and into the 1930s that legislation extinguished the convict lease system, apparently in response to pressure from rural manufacturers and labor unions who could not stand the competition, especially with the coming of the Depression.

Even the central idea of how prisons ought to be shaped was formulated by persons who wanted to create prisons for profit. It is well-known that Jeremy Bentham designed the Panopticon, the building which so to speak symbolizes total control. 'Pan opticon' means total view. Bentham's invention is built as a huge shell in a circle with a tall tower in the middle. In the external circle are the cells. They have windows facing both in and out. In the tower in the middle are the guards. From their position they can see through every cell and observe everything without being seen themselves. It provided for maximum surveillance at a minimum cost. Jeremy Bentham also planned tubes so the sounds from each cell could be monitored.

Bentham designed and developed plans for private contractors to run his institution. What is more, according to Feeley (1991a, pp. 4–5), Bentham "campaigned tirelessly to obtain this contract for himself, believing that it would make him a wealthy man ... From the early 1780s until the early 1800s, he was obsessed with this idea. He invested thousands of pounds of his own money in efforts to acquire a site and to develop a prototype of the Panopticon."

He lost his investment. But his basic design became influential, both architecturally and economically.

Feeley's conclusion from the history of privatization is that:

> ... when the state is faced with demands it cannot meet, entrepreneurs can and do help develop a response, ultimately enlarging the state's capacities. As with transportation, early private prison contractors responded to a widely-felt crisis, developed innovative solutions and quickly implemented them. That their inventions were modified or absorbed by the state does not indicate failure but success.

The other part of the great American tradition came from the import of *slaves* from Africa. No official record was kept of the slave trade. Gunnar Myrdal (1964, pp. 118–119) estimates that it is likely that the total number of slaves imported into the United States before 1860 was under a million. Federal law prohibited the slave trade in 1808. At that time, between 300,000 and 400,000 had arrived. But more slaves were added through annexations of territory, and most of all by smuggling slaves into the country. A good many of the Negro slaves who were liberated after the Civil War were African-born. Today there are 15 million black males in the USA.

Close to half of the prison population in the USA is black. Marc Mauer has in two reports (1991 and 1992) calculated the figures for black male inmates, and moreover compared them with the situation in South Africa. We give his figures in our *Table 7.8-1*. Half a million black males are now in prison or jail. This means that 3,400 per 100,000 – or 3.4 per cent – of the male black population are in prison just now. How extreme this is, internationally, can be seen when it is compared with South Africa, where 681 per 100,000 black males – or 0.7 per cent – are incarcerated.

Table 7.8-1 Black Male Rates Of Incarcerations in USA and South Africa 1989 and 1990

	United States	South Africa
Black Male Population 1989	14,625,000	15,050,642
Black Male Inmates 1989	454,724	109,739
Rate of Incarceration per 100,000 1989	3,109	729
Black Male Inmates 1990	499,871	107,202
Rate of Incarceration per 100,000 1990	3,370	681

From Mauer (1992), Table 2.

With 3.4 per cent in prison, one and a half times as many are probably on probation or parole, which means that between seven and eight per cent of black males are under some sort of legal constraint.

Again, this is a conservative estimate. Blumstein (1991, p. 53) has this to say:

> ... if you focus on the highest risk group – black males in their '20s – the incarceration rate is about 4,200, or about 4.2 percent of the group. That means that almost one of every 20 black males in his '20s is in a state or federal prison today. Adding the local jails, which comprise another 50 percent, we are up to 6.3 percent, which is the fraction of black males in their '20s in the United States who are in either a state or federal prison or a local jail. When you recognize that prison represents about one-sixth of the total number of people under control of the criminal justice system (including probation and parole), you can then multiply the prior number (the 4.2 percent) by six and that comes to about 25 percent.

25 per cent, that means every fourth black man in his '20s. But this is for the country as a whole. If we also concentrated on youth in the inner cities, it is highly probable that we, according to Blumstein's estimates, would have to conclude that considerably more than this quarter of the black male population was under the control of the criminal justice system at any time.

With all this in mind, it is easy to understand that Marc Mauer (1991, p. 9) formulates one of his sub-titles in his report like this:

AFRICAN-AMERICAN MALES: AN ENDANGERED SPECIES?

And Mauer continues:

> African-American males, who are disproportionately low-income, face a variety of problems, including: the social and economic decline of our inner cities and diminished opportunities for young people; the continuing failure of our schools, health care systems, and other institutional supports to prepare young Black males to occupy legitimate roles in society; continuing poverty and a distribution of wealth which has resulted in even greater disparity between the rich and the poor over the past twenty years.

And this over-representation of blacks is steadily increasing. Austin and McVey (1989, p. 5) point to the war against drugs as one important explanation:

Drug enforcement has been narrowly focused on crack, the drug of choice among the underclass, which is also disproportionately Black and Hispanic. Consequently, the proportion of offenders sentenced to prison who are non-white is escalating.

Mauer points to the same:

From 1984 to 1988, the Black community's percentage of all drug arrests nationally increased from 30 percent to 38 percent. In Michigan, drug arrests overall have doubled since 1985, while drug arrests of Blacks have tripled. With a "war on drugs" primarily waged through the criminal justice system and disproportionally targeting inner-city users, the end result is an increasing number of prisoners and an ever larger share of Black inmates.

Florida is probably the most extreme among states in this regard. In 1982/1983, there were 299 felony drug cases brought against male juveniles in Florida. There were 54 cases against black juveniles. In 1985, the numbers for whites was 336, while the blacks had now – with the figure 371 – passed the whites. But then, in 1989/90 , the numbers of blacks had increased to 3415, while whites were lagging far behind with only 526.[2] The architect behind this growth, Governor Marinez, lost the election for a new period as Governor, but has instead become the drug-czar for the whole country.

It does not seem unreasonable to think that the combination of being black and poor is a handicap at the court-level as well, although this is debated (cf. the discussion between Wilbanks and Mann 1987). Personally, I have never been able to forget the results in a little study by Wolfgang, Kelly and Nolde as far back as 1962. They compared prisoners admitted to death row. According to all probability, black people came into this queue with greater ease – that means for somewhat less good reasons – than white people. As a result, one might have expected that a relatively smaller quota of black people would eventually be executed after having gone through the various appeal procedures. But the results were the opposite. Relatively more blacks

2 From Florida Supreme Court Racial and Ethnic Bias Commission, 1991.

than whites were killed. Mauer's last report (1992, pp. 11–12) gives several examples of general mechanisms working in the disfavour of blacks in the legal process.

But let me add: European prisons have also darkened. And if poverty had colour, they would have darkened even more. There is no reason for European chauvinism vis à vis the USA. Both class and race are reflected in the figures on black prisoners from the USA. And both in Australia and in Canada there exists extreme over-representation of ethnic minority groups in prison.

7.9 The standard setter

There are no "natural limits" in the perception of what is a large prison population. With the growth in the USA, standards of size change. In a world so influenced by what happens in the USA, this may have an impact all over the industrialized world. Maybe we are unduly lenient in Europe, since the USA seems to thrive with ten times as many prisoners? Ideas of privatization have also crossed the Atlantic. Sir Edward Gardner(1989) was the chairman of the Parliamentary All Party Select Committee on Home Affairs. He took the Committee to the USA, and had this to say on his return:

> ... all of us, who went over to America to look at these new establishments, wondered if we were wasting our time; in my diary I wrote that this was a proposition that looked more absurd than real. But as members of the Committee went around these institutions in places like Memphis, Panama and Nashville, I can only tell you that we began radically to change our minds. We were astonished by what we saw – the quality of the management and the success of the whole idea of private prisons.

Sir Edward actually changed his views to the extent that he – when he gave his lecture at the Institute for the Study and Treatment of Delinquency – had become the chairman of the private firm "Contract Prisons PLC".

And he is not alone. Taylor and Peace (1989) make a plea for using this opportunity for reform. The crucial question, they say, is not whether a prison is run for profit, but whether acceptable and relevant standards are applied. Among these, they specify that no private contract should be for a period in excess of five years, after which competitive tender would recur. Furthermore, the private prisons should not be allowed to receive only the easy ones – no one serving less than 18 months would be eligible. And most important: a conviction-free period after release will be a tacit objective and will form the basis of part of the payment. They argue (p. 192) that if prison privatization takes place as an unthinking copy of North Amerrican practice, the situation in U.K. will probably become worse. And they conclude:

> In short, the potential advantages which prisons offer are specific to a narrow range of possible schemes. Our advocacy of such schemes is therefore a high-risk strategy. If all the right elements are not in place, ...we will have opened our gates to a particularly unpleasant Trojan Horse.

It is difficult to disagree.

But this perspective of US influence on the rest of the world may be too narrow. It is not only a question of whether what happens in the USA today will happen in the UK and Canada tomorrow. According to Lilly and Knepper (1991), privatization is not a one-way flow of penal policies from the US to the UK:

> ... the relationship between the two nations is not based on the transfer of correctional policy so much as it is on the joint ownership of corporations ...[3]

> The relation between the UK and the US involves corporations joining forces to market corrections products and services in both countries. Rather than implementing only US correctional policies in the UK, some British companies have purchased a stake in the US corrections

---

3 Consider the electronic monitoring market. Electronic monitoring of offenders has generated significant commercial interest. In 1987, three American vendors – BI Incorporated, Correctional Services Incorporated and Digital Products – controlled the market in electronic tagging devices. Since then, two US vendors have combined with British companies to produce and market an improved device....And in 1989 Corrections Services, Inc. again expanded its international business connections with Japanese-based Mitsubishi; in 1990 C.S.I. further expanded its international business dealings with an agreement with Electron Dart, Ltd. in Tel Aviv, Israel.(Lilly and Knepper pp. 15-16).

market. Whether or not private prisons appear on a wide scale in the UK, its firms will continue to profit from punishments in the US, the largest corrections market.

Some final comments on the industrial drive: If the level and form of control in society is shaped by features of the social organization, it may well be that these general features will manifest themselves everywhere. The total number of prisoners in Europe has also increased during the last years. *Diagram 7.9-1* illustrates what has happened. And the Netherlands itself has increased its prison population. As described in *Chapter 4*, the solutions in countries with a low level of prisoners are under strong pressures these days. Particularly important are the developments in drug policy – again with the USA as trend-setter. Of importance also are recent trends in the mass-media. With crime as major content, it is not easy to hold the old line. In

Diagram 7.9-1. Developments in the number of prisoners in Council of Europe member States since 1970 excluding Austria, Iceland, the Netherlands, Switzerland and Turkey

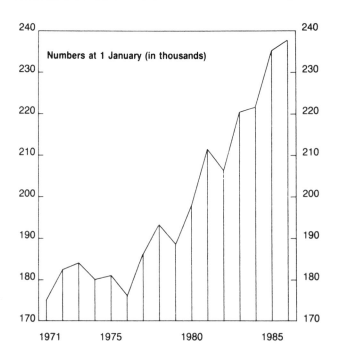

addition come two other factors: *the capacity* for modern industrial society to institutionalize large segments of the population, and also that such a solution *would be in harmony with important other trends in these nations.* This will be the theme of the next chapter.

Chapter 8

Modernity in decisions

8.1 4,926 applicants

I had some problems the other day, but only small ones. We have a selection committee for applicants to the Faculty of Law at my university. I am a member. Once a year we decide on the major intake of new students. There were 4,926 applicants this summer. 500 were to be admitted. Youth unemployment has put immense pressure on the system of higher education. But for us the task was simple. Most decisions on admissions are made on the basis of grades in high school. The grades are added up into one major figure. Some additional points may be included for various types of work experience. A conscientious and highly efficient secretary prepares it all and ranks the applicants. The committee is left with the task of deciding the cut-off point. All applicants above that point are admitted.

But we have two additional problems. Some applicants ask for extra-ordinary admission for health and social reasons. Maybe they had a severe illness or a death in the family during their final exams, or maybe they were deaf or blind, confined to wheelchairs, or had severe problems with drugs, crime or general mental instability. We discuss each case, and admit most of them. The faculty has to take its share of those in trouble. But at the same time, and in miniature, we face the general welfare problem: Is it right to make it as easy to enter the university via prison or mental hospital as through hard work and good grades from school? Mostly, we have said yes. Luckily, there have not been many such applicants.

Another category also creates problems, not because of the individual applicants, but because of the type of school they come from. Those schools stubbornly refuse to grade their students according to the official grading scale. They insist that final exams and grades do not tell us enough about the pupils. Instead, each teacher at these schools writes a small essay about every pupil in every subject, and adds to this a detailed evaluation of one major piece of work the pupil has accomplished; a painting, a photo exhibition, an essay on Sartre, a reconstruction of an ancient pair of skis from the valley....

This is impossible – for the selection committee. We had three applicants from those schools this year. I remember them all, inevitably, they come so close. All of them are from the so-called Waldorf Schools, or Rudolf Steiner schools as they are called in Scandinavia. Pupils there have often had the same teachers for 12 years in school. The teachers know them, perhaps too well. Often they write about their pupils with deep insight, and mostly with love. They have been close to their students, and bring them close to us. It makes the task of decision-makers impossible.

Three applicants without grades. And a few "social cases". These were the applicants I got to know . But there were at least 4,400 other applicants who were not admitted. Young people with all sorts of qualities and all sorts of needs for admission. But their qualifications had been converted into numbers, and their numbers were wrong.

To make matters worse – and this is very relevant to my topic of the potentialities of Modernity, I am – for many reasons of principle – against exams and the grading of pupils. I have been an active member of a Royal Commission which proposed the abolition of grades in our compulsory school system. And even worse, I am also against limited admission to universities and have voted against it several times. But I have lost my cases, and feel obliged to participate in the administrative tasks given me. If I had not done it, someone else would have. Maybe I rescue one or two who otherwise would not be admitted to the holy land.

8.2 Bottlenecks

One reason why justice takes so long is that the courts are overburdened with work and poorly equipped to cope with it. This is common knowledge. Time has somehow passed many courts by. The wigs are mostly gone, but not the slow pace. Typewriters have replaced goose quills, and some courts have computers, but by and large, the courts remain bottlenecks, unable to adapt to demands. In addition, their output does not stand up to quality control. Numerous studies show great disparities in sentencing. The same acts result in months of imprisonment in one district and years in another. This creates extra work for the appeal courts, or injustice if not appealed.

In the USA, this is all now about to be changed. Much has already been done.

In 1984, Congress enacted the Sentencing Reform Act. The basic objective of the Act was to enhance the ability of the criminal justice system to combat crime through an efficient and fair sentencing system. Fair meant particularly less disparity. The same acts were to be met with the same punishments. For that purpose, the reform gave both more and less powers to the courts. It gave more power by abolishing the earlier system of indeterminate sentences and parole boards which decided on releases. Time for release would now be decided by the courts. But it also gave less power, by establishing a system of detailed instructions on the sentence in each individual case.

For that purpose, Congress established the United States Sentencing Commission. This is

> an independent agency in the judicial branch composed of seven voting and two non-voting, ex officio members. Its principal purpose is to establish sentencing policies and practices for the federal criminal justice system that will assure the ends of justice by promulgating detailed guidelines prescribing the appropriate sentences for offenders convicted of federal crimes. (U.S. Sentencing Commission Guidelines 1990, p. 1.1).

In a decision (Misretta v. United States) the Supreme Court of the United States upheld the constitutionality of the Sentencing Commis-

Table 8.3-1. Sentencing Table (in months of imprisonment)
Criminal History Category (Criminal History Points)

Offense Level	I (0 or 1)	II (2 or 3)	III (4, 5, 6)	IV (7, 8, 9)	V (10, 11, 12)	VI (13 or more)
1	0-6	0-6	0-6	0-6	0-6	0-6
2	0-6	0-6	0-6	0-6	0-6	0-6
3	0-6	0-6	0-6	0-6	0-6	0-6
4	0-6	0-6	0-6	2-8	4-10	6-12
5	0-6	0-6	1-7	4-10	6-12	9-15
6	0-6	1-7	2-8	6-12	9-15	12-18
7	1-7	2-8	4-10	8-14	12-18	15-21
8	2-8	4-10	6-12	10-16	15-21	18-24
9	4-10	6-12	8-14	12-18	18-24	21-27
10	6-12	8-14	10-16	15-21	21-27	24-30
11	8-14	10-16	12-18	18-24	24-30	27-33
12	10-16	12-18	15-21	21-27	27-33	30-37
13	12-18	15-21	18-24	24-30	30-37	33-41
14	15-21	18-24	21-27	27-33	33-41	37-46
15	18-24	21-27	24-30	30-37	37-46	41-51
16	21-27	24-30	27-33	33-41	41-51	46-57
17	24-30	27-33	30-37	37-46	46-57	51-63
18	27-33	30-37	33-41	41-51	51-63	57-71
19	30-37	33-41	37-46	46-57	57-71	63-78
20	33-41	37-46	41-51	51-63	63-78	70-87
21	37-46	41-51	46-57	57-71	70-87	77-96
22	41-51	46-57	51-63	63-78	77-96	84-105
23	46-57	51-63	57-71	70-87	84-105	92-115
24	51-63	57-71	63-78	77-96	92-115	100-125
25	57-71	63-78	70-87	84-105	100-125	110-137
26	63-78	70-87	78-97	92-115	110-137	120-150
27	70-87	78-97	87-108	100-125	120-150	130-162
28	78-97	87-108	97-121	110-137	130-162	140-175
29	87-108	97-121	108-135	121-151	140-175	151-188
30	97-121	108-135	121-151	135-168	151-188	168-210
31	108-135	121-151	135-168	151-188	168-210	188-235
32	121-151	135-168	151-188	168-210	188-235	210-262
33	135-168	151-188	168-210	188-235	210-262	235-293
34	151-188	168-210	188-235	210-262	235-293	262-327
35	168-210	188-235	210-262	235-293	262-327	292-365
36	188-235	210-262	235-293	262-327	292-365	324-405
37	210-262	235-293	262-327	292-365	324-405	360-life
38	235-293	262-327	292-365	324-405	360-life	360-life
39	262-327	292-365	324-405	360-life	360-life	360-life
40	292-365	324-405	360-life	360-life	360-life	360-life
41	324-405	360-life	360-life	360-life	360-life	360-life
42	360-life	360-life	360-life	360-life	360-life	360-life
43	life	life	life	life	life	life

sion against several challenges, so by now the Commission claims to be the determining factor at the Federal level with regard to penal law in the USA.

8.3 Manuals for decisions on pain

One of the major results of the work of the Sentencing Commission is reproduced in *Table 8.3-1*. This is a so-called Sentencing Table. The basic principle for the use of the table is simple enough. Let us first look at some examples of offence levels, the vertical column on the left. The task of the judge here is to decide the type of crime. The crime may be Aircraft Piracy, or Attempted Aircraft Piracy. The Manual, section 2.14 , is clear.

> a) Base Offence Level: 38
> b) If death resulted, increase by 5 levels

If death resulted, the offender ends up with 38 + 5 = 43, which is said to mean "life" in the table.

A more complex case would be Burglary of a Residence. The instructions on this read:

> Burglary of a Residence
> (a) Base Offence Level:...........17
> (b) Specific Offence Characteristics
>
> (1) If the offence involved more than minimal planning, increase by 2 levels.
> (2) If the loss exceeded $ 2,500, increase the offense level as follows:

Loss (Apply the Greatest)	Increase in Level
A) $2,500 or less	no increase
(B) More than $2,500	add 1
(C) More than $10,000	add 2
(D) More than $50,000	add 3
(E) More than $250,000	add 4
(F) More than $800,000	add 5
(G) More than $1,500,000	add 6
(H) More than $2,500,000	add 7
(I) More than $5,000,000	add 8.

(3) If a firearm, destructive device, or controlled substance was taken, or if the taking of such item was an object of the offense, increase by 1 level.

(4) If a dangerous weapon (including a firearm) was possessed, increase by 2 levels.

As we see, the minimum level of punishment would be 17. In the worst case, the maximum is 30.

By this, half the job is done. The remainder is to determine the Criminal History Category. Section 4.1 in the Manual tells how:

(a) Add 3 points for each prior sentence of imprisonment exceeding one year and one month.

(b) Add 2 points for each prior sentence of imprisonment of at least sixty days not counted in(a).

(c) Add 1 point for each prior sentence not included in (a) or (b), up to a total of 4 points for this item.

(d) Add 2 points if the defendant committed the instant offence while under any criminal justice sentence, including probation, parole, supervised release, imprisonment, work release, or escape status.

(e) Add 2 points if the defendant committed the instant offence less than two years after release from imprisonment on a sentence counted under (a) or (b) or while in imprisonment or escape status on such a sentence. If 2 points are added for item (d), add only 1 point for this item.

The maximum in the sentencing table is 13 points. Four earlier sentences exceeding 13 months of imprisonment, and one minor sentence, produce that result.

With these instructions, we could all do the job.

A burglary took place (level 17), well planned (increase to level 19), and resulted in the loss of more than $ 10,000 (increase to level 21), but no guns or drugs were stolen and firearms were not used, so we end down the vertical scale at offence level 21.

The offender had been sentenced twice before to more than 13 months of imprisonment, so his Criminal History Category along the horizontal scale is 6. We go down from that point until we meet the horizontal line from level 21, and the result is clear: The judge is free to choose a prison sentence of between 46 and 57 months.

A bottleneck has been removed.

8.4 Purified justice

The advantage of such a Manual is its honesty. It makes clear what it includes, but also what has been excluded. Congress has been quite specific in its instructions to the Commission on this point. It:

> requires the Commission to assure that its guide-lines and policy state-ments reflect the general inappropriateness of considering the defen-dant's education, vocational skills, employment record, family ties and responsibilities, and community ties in determining whether a term of imprisonment should be imposed or the length of a term of imprison-ment.(The Manual, p. 5.35)

I must confess I had to read twice: Inappropriateness? In my tradition I would have expected a requirement to let the Manual reflect the *appropriateness* of considering all those factors. But that is not the case, and the Commission follows this up with specific orders *not* to consider:

> Age.
> Education and Vocational Skills.
> Mental and Emotional Conditions.
> Physical Conditions, Including Drug Dependence and Alcohol Abuse.
> Previous Employment Record.
> Family Ties and Responsibilities, and
> Community Ties.
> Race, Sex, National Origin, Creed, Religion and Social Economic Sta-tus.(The Manual, pp. 5.35–5.37).

To someone used to the old-fashioned European crime policy tradi-tion, these directives are surprising, to put it mildly. On a kind inter-pretation, the decision to exclude some of these factors may be thought to reflect an attempt to achieve a different sort of justice. Congress may have feared that those who met the right criteria might receive preferential treatment simply for that reason. Upper-class criminals might point to family and community ties as well as to important responsibilities, and thereby unjustly escape punishments given to persons without those ties and responsibilities.

The person who is rich in money and social ties should not thanks to that good fortune escape the full burden of punishment. Fine. But what about persons without ties and responsibilities and with extremely low social status? By preventing the courts from considering all these factors – so as not to give extra advantages to the already privileged – they at the same time block the possibility to show extra leniency towards the particularly disadvantaged. They eliminate the whole question of social justice. What about the very poor offender, who steals out of hunger, or the lonely person, with no social ties at all? To prevent abuse by the (few) well-off persons, the legislators make it illegal for the justice to take into consideration precisely those factors which most of the prison population have as their common background: poverty and deprivation, the absence of a share in the good life, all those key attributes of the non-productive "dangerous class".

If Congress had wanted to ensure that those who were well off socially and economically would not obtain advantages, it could have solved the problem. It is no more complex to operationalize social factors than to operationalize acts which are interpreted as crimes. Let me help the Commission with the following proposed Offence Level scale:

First some points on *increases:*

> Offenders with high educations (who therefore ought to have known better), add 2 points

> Offenders with an annual income the last two years over X dollars, add 4 points

> Offenders with earlier solid social networks and responsibilities, add 5 points

And then as to *reductions:*

> Offenders without the minimum compulsory education, deduct 3 points
>
> Offenders defined as living below the poverty level, deduct 4 points
>
> Offenders with extraordinary traumas in youth and insufficient social backgrounds according to a social investigation, deduct 5 points

The list could have been larger, and the weighting heavier. How much culpability is left in a female beaten and sexually abused by her father from childhood, living in misery and poverty – who then in despair kills that father? Or, not to make it too obvious: what about a case where in addition her mother knew about it all without interfering? What weight as a mitigating circumstance should be given to all this, and maybe in addition to having been brought up in a slum? Might it not happen, that when all mitigating factors were added, some culprits would have to be moved *below* Offence Level 1, so that the judge would be obliged to sentence society to give them compensation? To go deep into these matters would mean destroying crime control as a useful theme in the political debate – for those participating in that debate.

Radzinowicz and Hood (1981) describe the development leading up to this situation. So much of the reform stemmed from honest wishes for reduced use of imprisonment. The influential *Committee for the Study of Incarceration* (von Hirsch 1976) was quite explicit in favour of the imposition of less, not more punishment. To abandon the rehabilitative model without a simultaneous gradation downwards in prison sentences would, according to the committee, be an unthinkable cruelty and a dangerous act. Five years, save for murder, would be the highest penalty. Radzinowicz and Hood also quote (p. 142) former Chief Judge Bazelon (1978):

> (He) hits the nail on the head when he castigates the Senate's Bill proposing the establishment of a Commission, on the grounds that under the rhetoric of equality it "envisions the criminal process as a vast engine of social control". As the problem of crime is embedded in the social conditions of a society "so judgments must be made within the rich context of an offender's background". The attempt to "automate" this delicate process "deprives participants, and the public itself, of the information that is essential to our concept of criminal justice".

Reasons for not including social factors in the sentencing table are solidly based in the ideology of *just deserts*. The main content of this idea is that punishments ought to reflect the blameworthiness of criminal acts. And the less social factors are included in the account, the clearer the relation becomes between the concrete act and the punishment. Social factors obfuscate the clear and supposedly justly deserved punishment resulting from the evil act. In the framework of just deserts, this is seen as harmful. The moral scale – and the clarity of the message to the population – is blurred. So is the possibility of preventing injustice, in the sense of different punishments for the same acts. The goal is to prevent inequality, but the social consequences are that other important values are squeezed out of the system of decision. Just deserts become just in one sense, but highly unjust where several values ought to be weighed against each other. Since these other values mostly would have counted to the advantage of the disadvantaged, the limitations in just deserts create – in totality – an extremely unjust system. By virtue of its simplicity, it becomes a most useful theory for fast justice and a depersonalization of the offender during the penal process.

8.5 Offender cooperation

According to the Bill of Rights, all Americans accused of crime have the right to a trial by an impartial jury. In the world of realities, hardly any of the accused use this right. More than 90 per cent – in some jurisdictions as many as 99 per cent – plead guilty. If not, if guilty pleas were reduced by even a small percentage, the whole system of courts in the USA would be completely paralyzed.

But why do they plead guilty?

Because they cannot take the risk of pleading not guilty.

The mechanism to assure this fabulous offender cooperation is called plea bargaining. It is simple enough. The prosecutor believes that he can prove that the supposed offender has committed the acts A, B, C and D. He then promises that he will only charge the supposed offender with acts A and B *if the offender pleads guilty to these acts.*

Americans are in this way not sentenced for what they have done, but for what they have agreed with the prosecutor to reveal in court.

The Sentencing Commission did not like the system, and tried to abolish plea bargaining[1]. But they gave it up, among other things because they did not:

> find a practical way to reconcile the need for a fair adjudicating procedure with the need for a speedy sentencing process... (p. 1.5).

So, when a judge uses the sentencing table, the act to be categorized is not what it has been proved that the offender has done, but what the offender and the prosecutor have agreed to say that the offender has done, – if he is so kind as to confess and thereby assure a simple and fast session in court.

Langbein (1978) points to two consequences of such a system. First, it concentrates enormous power on the side of the prosecution (p. 18):

> Our formal law of trial envisages a division of responsibility. We expect the prosecutor to make the charging decision, the judge and especially the jury to adjudicate, and the judge to set the sentence. Plea bargaining merges these accusatory, determinative, and sanctional phases of the procedure in the hands of the prosecutor.

Radzinowicz and Hood agree completely (1981, pp. 142–143):

> A drastic restriction of the discretionary powers of the judiciary and its supervision by a commission will reduce the judge's role in the criminal process and increase the power of public prosecutors.

---

1 The Commission writes (p.1.4 – 1.5):

> One of the most important questions for the Commission to decide was whether to base sentences upon the actual conduct in which the defendant engaged regardless of the charges for which he was indicted or convicted ("real offence" sentencing), or upon the conduct that constitutes the elements of the offence for which the defendant was charged and of which he was convicted ("charge offence" sentencing). A bank robber, for example, might have used a gun, frightened bystanders, taken $50,000, injured a teller, refused to stop when ordered, and raced away damaging property during his escape. A pure real offence system would sentence on the basis of all identifiable conduct. A pure offence system would overlook some of the harms that did not constitute statute elements of the offences of which the defendant was convicted.

But to become able to force the offender to confess, something terrible has to happen if he does not confess. In Langbein's words (p. 12):

> In twentieth-century America we have duplicated the central experience of medieval European criminal procedure: we have moved from an adjudicatory to a confessionary system. We coerce the accused against whom we find probable cause to confess his guilt. To be sure, our means are much politer; we use no rack, no thumb-screw, no Spanish boot to mash his legs. But like the Europeans of distant centuries who did employ those machines, we make it terribly costly for an accused to claim his right to the constitutional safeguard of trial. We threaten him with a materially increased sanction if he avails himself of his right and is thereafter convicted. The sentencing differential is what makes plea bargaining coercive.

And in a footnote (p. 17) he raises the question whether the plea bargaining system is responsible for the high punishment level of the USA. He states:

> In the nineteenth and twentieth centuries, when the Europeans were ameliorating their sentences, we were not. It is tempting to wonder whether the requirements of the plea bargaining system have been somewhat responsible.

8.6 Depersonalization

A political decision to eliminate concern for the social background of the defendant involves much more than making these characteristics inappropriate for decisions on pain. By the same token, the offender is to a large extent excluded as a person. There is no point in exposing a social background, childhood, dreams, defeats, – perhaps mixed with some glimmer from happy days – social life, all those small things which are essential to a perception of the other as a full human being. With the Sentencing Manual and its prime outcome, the Sentencing Table, crime is standardized as Offence Levels, a person's life as Criminal History Points, and decisions on the delivery of pain are reduced to finding the point where two lines merge. The right decision becomes a point in space, and pain.

The penal process thus acquires a similarity to what Georg Simmel (here l950) describes from economic life. To him, money becomes the condensed, anti-individualistic unit that makes modern life possible. His concern is that modernity destroys autonomy and individuality.

> ... the individuality of phenomena is not commensurate with the pecuniary principle.
> ... These traits must also colour the contents of life and favour the exclusion of those irrational, instinctive, sovereign traits and impulses which aim at determining the mode of life from within, instead of receiving the general and precisely schematized form of life from without (pp. 409–413).

For sentencing purposes, the defendant might as well not have been in court. Everything relates to the act, and to former acts defined as crimes. The offender has minimal opportunities to present her/himself as a usual and therefore peculiar member of the universe of humanity.

This decision-making system has the obvious consequence of creating distance from the person to be sentenced. When social attributes are eliminated, a seemingly "objective" and impersonal system is created. Harm is the monetary unit, – harm with pain as its price. It is a system in full accord with normal bureaucratic standards, and at the same time extraordinarily well suited for power-holders.

Distance can be created physically by a long-range gun, socially by class, professionally by a trained incapacity to see the whole person as he would have been seen as neighbour, friend or lover. In an authority structure additional distance is created by acting according to orders. The Sentencing Table is such an order from above. The judge might be a soft one. He might sense a life in misery. But the Table is there. I am so sorry, but your offence-level is 38. This is not my personal decision, I just have to carry it out.

With this system of sentencing, the authorities will have considerably more control than before. A system for the registration of all decisions on sentencing has been developed, and more is to come (United States Sentencing Commission Annual Report 1989). This moves power one step up the ladder, one step away from possible identification with the offender, and one step closer to the central authorities.

Sentencing Commissions have now been established in several states in the USA: Minnesota, Oregon, Pennsylvania and Washington. Minnesota is generally seen as a highly successful case (e.g.von Hirsch 1982), while Tonry (1991, p. 309) calls the Federal one a disaster. But the basic principles behind their work seem to be the same. They create their simplistic tables based on types of crime and numbers of earlier convictions, and the answer is given.[2]

2 In a paper with the grim title "Penal Regressions", Radzinowicz (1991a) has this to say:

> I regard Sentencing Commissions as having total flaws of one kind or another. They should not be regarded as a solution to the problems which face contemporary sentencing policy. ... To advise – yes, but not to direct (p. 434).

Chapter 9

Justice done, or managed?

Jokes in the *New Yorker* are sometimes incomprehensible to Europeans. We do not share the cultural background and do not always understand the symbols and their double meaning. Cultural symbols can only be understood in a context of shared experience.

To most people in our time, and on both sides of the Atlantic, the image of Lady Justice is familiar and packed with meaning. In one hand she holds scales, of course of an old fashioned type, based on the principle of balance. In the other she has a sword. Mostly she is blindfolded, and represented in white clothes.

This symbol is of great importance, but of course not to all people. Perhaps we can understand law better if we look at social systems where she is of no importance at all, and compare these with systems where she has a virtually sacred meaning. Let us do so by comparing three types of legal organization: Village Law, Representative Law, and Independent Law. This will be an ideal-typical description, an attempt to clarify some general principles behind legal arrangements.

9.1 Village law

… would be one where the symbol of Justice would have no meaning.

First, why should she be blindfolded in the village? Imagine a village with sufficient autonomy to decide on internal conflicts, with a long history – at least long enough to have established norms for what is right and what is wrong – and with relatively egalitarian relationships between people. In such a system, law would be a matter for all grown-ups living in the village. They would know the rules through participation. Even if legal decisions were to some extent formalized, the ownership of legal knowledge would not be monopolized. By living there, they would all know and would all be natural participants in the decision-making. These would not be simple decisions. Since there were no specialists, there would be no one with clear authority to delimit the volume or type of arguments. Discussions might last for days. Old histories would be renewed, earlier decisions brought forward.

In a very fundamental sense, such a village court would operate in close proximity to the villagers. Often all take part, all have relevant knowledge, and all have to live with the consequences of their decisions. But this description also makes it clear why Lady Justice is out of style in the village. Lady Justice is above everybody. She is in white, untouched and untouchable, not a part of the whole. And then blindfolded and with a sword in a situation where everything is relevant – where everything must be seen – and where a sword is impossible since that would mean conflicts which might destroy the village. Where authority is absent, consensus must be reached. The law of the village therefore tends towards civil solutions; compensations and compromises – not dichotomies of guilt/innocence and the delivery of pain to the loser.

These were the major features. But let me hasten to add: The law of the village would not necessarily be "just". In particular, it would give little protection to those without power and connections in the village. Females were often, but not always, in that position. It was a law for a time long since gone. But bits and pieces remain.

Reminiscences of the village tradition can be found in the term "justices of the peace". Where authority was neither strong nor distant, it was necessary to find solutions acceptable to the parties, to create peace. The closer decision-makers are to the participants in a conflict, the more important this becomes. With peace, the peace-maker gets both honour and a better life for himself in peaceful surroundings.

Peace-makers therefore know the importance of finding common ground. But the peace-makers cannot be blindfolded. On the contrary, she or he will need every sense to get a feeling of what might be common ground, where the parties might meet in a compromise. And a sword would be an absolutely impossible piece of equipment, as it symbolizes the possible use of force.

9.2 Representative law

In the village, the image of Lady Justice is irrelevant. She cannot be understood. But children of modernity may also have difficulty with that image, particularly if they are strong defenders of local democracy. According to many values, it is a matter of course that it is a good thing that the institution of law is close to the people. This can take two forms:

that judges and prosecutors are democratically elected,
or
that legislators have a strong influence on what happens in courts.

An operationalization of the first form is to put Lady Justice up for direct election, to get her into a position as an elected judge. This sounds democratic, and even more so if the district attorney and the chief of police are also up for election. If they do not act according to the wishes of the electorate, they may be thrown out of office at the next election.

But why then, make Lady Justice blindfolded? It would be a self-contradiction to bring her close to the people, but blind to their arguments. The idea behind blindfolding justice is of course to make her objective, to prevent her from seeing and being influenced by what she is not supposed to see. But to be democratically elected means that Lady Justice can be dethroned if she does not decide as her electorate thinks. There is a built-in conflict here. A justice close to the people – even a justice ideally representing that people – is at the same time a justice under maximum control by that people. That is the village justice, where the image of Lady Justice had no place. But she is also out of place running in a modern election. To survive elections, she must both listen and see. Besides, in the realities of modern societies, to be democratically elected does not mean representing everybody. Down to 50 percent take part in elections. A victory means representing the majority of those casting their votes. Often this means representing 1/3, even down to 1/4 of the population, not the totality, and particularly not small enclaves which may differ from the majority in style and some basic values. Being close to the people therefore, in our types of society, means being close to only a segment of that population. At the same time it means being distant from situations where justice is left in peace to strike a balance between values of importance to the totality. This is particularly so in societies where strong influence is exerted by the mass media in combination with public opinion surveys. Mass media thrive on crime, and give a distorted picture of what it is all about. And the surveys reflect the resulting surface opinions, which in turn strengthen the tendencies in the media.

But Lady Justice is also an anachronism in the second form above, where what happens in court is controlled in minute detail by the legislature. Again, such control sounds fine, according to democratic ideals. All power to the people, therefore power to the legislature rather than to the judges.

And it is, of course, the task of the legislature to issue the laws, and has always been so in societies which see themselves as democracies. The real problem has to do with the level of specification of the laws issued by the legislature. A law may state:

theft is a crime which has to be punished,
or
theft is a crime which has to be punished by imprisonment for up to 3 years,
or
theft is a crime which has to be punished by imprisonment for from 2 to 3 years ,
or
theft of type 19 is a crime which has to be punished by imprisonment for 30 months.

The dean of Scandinavian penal law, Professor Johs. Andenæs, had this to say in a recent article (1991, p. 386, my translation):

> Personally, I am critical of the change in relationship between the legislature and the courts which a detailed regulation of the courts' use of punishments represents... In a political democracy, nothing can be said against the right of the legislators to make the basic choice of values, both as to what to criminalize and to the amount of punishment. But it is difficult at the level of legislature to create a concrete and realistic conception of the realities that the courts will meet in individual and concrete cases. It is a common experience that lay people react differently when they get to know the individual case than when they make general statements on crime and punishment. There is no reason to believe that this is not also true of parliamentarians.

Andenæs probably had his experience with lay judges in mind. It is often seen, and is confirmed in the literature, that these tend to be more lenient towards criminals than the trained judges. They may argue in general for a crime policy of stern measures, but then they make an exception for the offender they meet in their particular case. There is such an abundance of special circumstances in this case; basically the defendant was a decent person, not a "real" criminal; at least she or he had suffered so much through life that a stern sanction would have been most unjust.

Sentencing Tables created by Sentencing Commissions represent the extreme case of Representative Law. Sentencing is completely controlled by the politicians, and the judge is to the same extent made impotent at the sentencing stage. The judge has no freedom to consider the peculiar character of any case. Courts can decide on the concrete facts; did the defendant do it or not? But the whole question of mitigating and aggravating factors is removed from their domain. In this situation, Lady Justice does not need to be blindfolded. She has nothing to look at, except a Table. Central authorities in the form of a Sentencing Commission have decided. And there is no need for her scales. The weighing too, is done in the Table. The task has been simplified. No wonder things are speeding up, an advance for modernity. But her sword is easier to use than ever. A sword directed by a Table.

9.3 Independent law

Children come to some sort of agreement on rules. They learn them through making. Villagers in small scale systems inherit the basic principles of the legal system, but then – in a process of general participation – continue the game. Their discussion is one of norm clarification. Slowly, the whole complicated case is brought into the daylight. Arguments are sorted out, accepted or rejected, given weight, and added up. The process is more than a mere weighing in the scalepans of Justice. It is a process of repeatedly going into the facts, and then comparing facts with norms. What takes place is a sort of value-crystallization, a clarification to everybody of the basic values of the system.

Old-fashioned courts still have their roots in this tradition. A judge is not free as a child to decide the rules, nor as relatively free as a villager. This sort of judge is guided by law, and by training if he is a professional judge. But some room exists, some room for the unexpected, for those concerns no one had thought of before they were made obvious by being formulated.

But basically, this is undemocratic. Judges of this type are not close to the people, as in the village, or directed by the people, as in the case of representative law. Independent judge is the term we use. That independence may vary. The most extreme independence comes when judges get the job from a selecting body of other judges, when they have their task for life, when the whole process of appeal remains in their hands, and when they are protected from the rest of society by wealth and/or rank.

It is easy to understand the democratic criticism of this type of judge. Detailed instructions from Parliament or Sentencing Commissions are one type of answer, one type of attempt to bring judges under control. Public opinion surveys are another. Such surveys can convey the views of the population which could be used as a standard for the right punishment. But the questions in polls do not go deep enough, and are in our time mostly pale reflections of stereotypes created by the media. Questionnaires are not answered under the burden of responsibility. Acts are the tests of opinions. Concrete acts. It is

JUSTICE DONE, OR MANAGED? **149**

through ordinary people's responsible participation in concrete cases of decisions on the use of pain that we get insights into their principles of justice. It is only when they personally have to decide on the use of pain, and preferably have to carry out the decision themselves, that we get to know the basic views emerging from the process of participation.

Perhaps we must accept that there is no way out. Maybe the old idea of some distance between the executive, legislative, and judicial powers has something to be said for it. And in this situation, the idea of Lady Justice acquires a meaning. The old-fashioned judge is a free person, but there are limits. Some fundamental values are supposed to be at the bottom of her or his reasoning. The decisions are not for sale. This is where the blindfolding of Lady Justice comes in. She must not be influenced by irrelevancies – money, connections, kinship. She has to stay clean – white, and she needs her scales. Her task is complicated. The central question in legal struggles has always had to do with what it is permissible to put onto her scales. First, what sort of arguments it is permissible to put on, and thereafter what weight those arguments can be given.

9.4 The silent revolution

No wonder modern managers often leave old-fashioned court rooms in disgust. They may be there as witnesses, as victims, or charged with a crime. And they meet the formalities: gowns, probably everybody rising when the judge enters, perhaps oaths with a hand on the Bible. Then the slow pace, the detailed documentation, the endless repetitions until it is all over – or so the manager thinks until he learns that it takes weeks, or even months before the verdict arrives.

It is easy to understand the manager's impatience. Compared to decision-making machineries of the type he knows from modern industry, the courts stand out as archaic. They are out of place in modern times, and must be changed.

Which is exactly what happens.

The American system of justice has been undergoing revolutionary development these last few years. But the country seems not to be quite aware of its own revolution. No wonder. The first industrial revolution arrived with noisy and smoky machinery, of which no one could remain unaware. The characteristic feature of modern production on the other hand, and of the present revolutionary process, is its silence. Most of it takes place at the symbolic level. Money is moved around by means of small signs conveyed electronically. To a large extent, the product is symbols, words, perspectives, new ways of conceiving life and organizing life. The recent revolution is gentle in appearance, peaceful, and promises comfort to many people.

On the legal side, the law and order system is quietly, but highly efficiently, adapting to modernity, adapting to becoming a child of industrialization. Central values here are the clarification of goals, production control, cost reduction, rationality, and the division of labour, all combined with the coordination of all actions at a higher level of command. We are back both to Max Weber and to a system of extreme efficiency in reaching those clearly defined goals.

As formulated in further written comments on this book from Flemming Balvig:

> The adaptation can be seen in the physical changes taking place within the court-rooms. Slowly, these rooms take the form of an office of a junior director in a large firm. Gone are the gowns. The old paintings on the wall are exchanged for modern lithographs, forms of expressions become more straight forward, the seating arrangements more similar to those for ordinary decision-makers. The computer gets a natural place in the room. The radiation of solemn power, old heritage and justice is exchanged for comfort and efficiency.

The adaptation can also be seen in the output of the penal system. Production is faster, many more people can be sentenced with much less effort than before. Decisions are more uniform. Similar acts seen as crimes are punished more equally. For those who define justice as equality, and equality as accomplished when all persons with the same criminal record and committing the same act are met with exactly the same type of intended pain, the level of justice has risen. Predictability within the system has also increased. Any child can read the Sentencing Table, find the Offence level of contemplated acts, and decide if it is worth it.

The major bottlenecks have been removed. Plea bargaining ensures fast confessions, and the sentencing manuals ensure fast decisions on punishment. This creates almost unlimited scope for processing cases. The manuals are bound to be computerised soon, if this has not already been done. With all the relevant factors built in, a secretary can prepare everything up to the point when the judge touches the final button giving the intervals of choice – and soon, no doubt, also the preferred alternative within the intervals.

Speed, accountability, similarity, clear messages to potential criminals, a system which offers easily operated control by central authorities in the form of a Sentencing Commission, which again is under the control of the elected representatives of the people, amounts to a perfect adaptation to modernity.

*

And once more: What happens in the USA also takes place elsewhere. Even England and Wales are on their way towards more central control of the judiciary. In a White Paper on Crime, Justice and Protecting The Public (Home Office 1990), the just deserts model is hailed. It comes as point 1 in the Summary of the main proposals from the Government:

> – a coherent legislative framework for sentencing, with the severity of the punishment matching the seriousness of the crime...

And then on pp. 1-2:

> The Court of Appeal has issued guidance, which the Government very much welcomes, for sentencing some of the more serious offences tried in the Crown Court. The Magistrates' Association has prepared provisional guidelines for cases tried in magistrates' courts. However, there is still too much uncertainty and little guidance about the principles which should govern sentencing. There is a similar uncertainty about the release of prisoners on parole.
>
> ...

The Government is therefore proposing a new and more coherent statutory framework for sentencing. It will build on the guidance already given by the Court of Appeal.

...

The aim of the Government's proposals is better justice through a more consistent approach to sentencing, so that convicted criminals get their "just deserts". The severity of the sentence of the court should be directly related to the seriousness of the offence.

But there are still limits to governmental interference in England and Wales (pp. 8–9):

The legislation will be in general terms. It is not the Government's intention that Parliament should bind the courts with strict legislative guidelines. The courts have shown great skill in the way they sentence exceptional cases. The courts will properly continue to have the wide discretion they need if they are to deal justly with the great variety of crimes which comes before them. The Government rejects a rigid statutory framework, on the lines of those introduced in the United States, or a system of minimum or mandatory sentences for certain offences. This would make it more difficult to sentence justly in exceptional cases. It would also result in more acquittals by juries, with more guilty men and women going free unjustly as a result.

So, two steps forward, and one back in England and Wales. But the position of an Attorney General is a new one in these countries. Through systematic appeals, that office will probably result in decreased variance in sentencing, and – it seems from the White Paper – represent a pressure in the direction of materializing ideas of just deserts. The Government also promises to make arrangements for training sentencers to give effect to the new sentencing policies and the more detailed interpretation of the legislation by the Court of Appeal. Furthermore:

The new legislative provisions, the maximum penalties for each offence, the guidance from the Court of Appeal and the Attorney General's new power to refer over-lenient sentences for very serious offenders to the Court of Appeal, should all contribute to the development of coherent sentencing practice, which can be disseminated to the courts by the Judicial Studies Board. Against *this* (italics mine) background, the Government sees no need for a Sentencing Council to develop sentencing policies or guidance.

May be the step back was only a half one.

9.5 Expressive behaviour

Modernity is rationality. But some aspects of crime go beyond ratio-nality. For the victim, the case – if it is a serious one – is most often a one-time occurrence. It is a highly loaded emotional affair. If the crime is perceived as a serious one, the victim may have feelings of anger, or even grief. No courts – except of the village type – are parti-cularly good at coping with such emotions. Most are dull and task-oriented. The victim is not a major character in the play; the case is directed by people claiming to represent the parties. This distance from the victim may be one reason for victim dissatisfaction and the many statements that criminals get away with their misdeeds too easily. Demands for stiffer penalties may be a result of lack of atten-tion to the needs of victims for expressive outlets, rather than of wishes for vengeance.

One way of correcting this would be to give the victim a more central position in the proceedings, while also attempting to reduce the uti-lity-oriented character of the whole operation. I have in other connec-tions tried to compare anger and grief (Christie 1987). Death is an occurrence which often results in extreme grief. At funerals it is legi-timate to express some of it. To my knowledge, nobody has – as yet – dared to tamper with this situation. There is no health-propaganda on the walls of the Crematorium: "If he had not smoked, we would not have been here today." Funerals may be one of the few remaining arenas for expressive behaviour.

Courts have for a long time been badly suited as expressive arenas. With modernity they move from bad to worse. Detailed instructions for sentencing, particularly computerized ones, may be as foreign to the sentencing process as they would be in the interaction between a sinner and a priest. Vengeance regulated by a table or by pressing a button represents one step further away from a situation where anger and grief are given legitimate outlets. The system has moved from expressive ritualism to managerial efficiency.

Some of the explosion in the US figures may relate to a sort of inter-institutional misunderstanding. The institution of the law has come too close to politics, at the same time as utility-thinking borrowed from the institution for production seems to have been given what appears to be absolute dominance.

Chapter 10

Brothers in control: penal law and psychiatry

10.1 A manual for decisions on mental disorders

As in penal law, so also in psychiatry. Also here they have a manual, in this case a manual for Decisions on Mental Disorders (DSM-III-R, 1987).

The psychiatric manual has several similarities to the one by the Sentencing Commission. They are similar in that both are large; the psychiatric one numbers 467 pages, the sentencing manual 687. They are also similar in the ways they came into being. Both manuals are products of long and tedious processes in large organizations close to political and professional power. The sentencing manual is a result of "grand politics" in the legislature, but also of professional debates as well as a bureaucratic process in the Commission itself. The manual on mental disorders is more a result of professional politics. The organizations behind the manuals are in both cases hierarchical. At the top of the manual of mental disorders is the American Psychiatric Association, in cooperation with the National Institute of Mental Health and also with the World Health Organization. Below them is the central work group, and further down some twenty-six advisory committees with over two hundred members selected on the basis of their expertise in particular areas.

In both cases great efforts were made to have broad segments of experts represented. From the outset the Sentencing Commission invested much energy in finding out what sorts of sentences were usually given for various crimes. They filed an enormous number of legal decisions, and calculated national trends. Those trends were then used as an important source for the sentencing manual. The statistical norm became the legal norm. The psychiatrists, on the other hand, relied more on the work of sub-committees. They were strongly oriented towards consensus (p. XX):

> Frequently, decisions made by an advisory committee had to be reconsidered when the details of the proposal were worked out by these smaller groups; in some cases, the advisory committee decisions were the result of a consensus that emerged among committee members. However, several controversies, particularly in the area of childhood, psychotic, anxiety, and sleep disorders, could be resolved only by actually polling committee members.

Thus, both manuals have a sort of empirical base. The Sentencing Commission used legal decisions as data, and established general standards on that basis. The psychiatrists established standards on the basis of decisions reached by the numerous committees. It is not surprising that both manuals, produced under such conditions, are a-theoretical, and explicitly so. The psychiatric manual finds theories impractical (p. XX iii):

> The major justification for the generally a-theoretical approach in DMS-III and DMS-III-R with regard to etiology is that the inclusion of etiologic theories would be an obstacle to use of the manual by clinicians of varying theoretical orientations, since it would not be possible to present all reasonable etiologic theories for each disorder.

But they add, politely (p. XXIV):

> It should be noted that DMS-III-R's generally a-theoretical approach to the classification and definition of mental disorders does not imply that theories about the etiology of the various mental disorders are unimportant in other contexts. In formulating treatment plans, many clinicians find it helpful to be guided by theories about etiology. Similarly, many research studies are designed to test various theories about the etiology of mental disorders.

*

Next, the contents: A natural starting point is the diagnostic criteria on p. 55 for conduct disorders:

A disturbance of conduct lasting at least six months, during which at least three of the following have been present

(1) has stolen without confrontation of a victim on more than one occasion (including forgery)
(2) has run away from home overnight at least twice while living in parental or parental surrogate home (or once without returning)
(3) often lies (other than to avoid physical or sexual abuse)
(4) has deliberately engaged in fire-setting
(5) is often truant from school (for older person, absent from work)
(6) has broken into someone else's house, building, or car
(7) has deliberately destroyed others' property (other than by fire-setting)
(8) has been physically cruel to animals
(9) has forced someone into sexual activity with him or her
(10) has used a weapon in more than one fight
(11) often initiates physical fights
(12) has stolen with confrontation of a victim (e.g., mugging, purse-snatching, extortion, armed robbery)
(13) has been physically cruel to people.

In a more general description, conduct disorder is described as follows (pp. 53–54):

> The essential feature of this disorder is a persistent pattern of conduct in which the basic rights of others and major age-appropriate societal norms or rules are violated. The behaviour pattern typically is present in the home, at school, with peers, and in the community. The conduct problems are more serious than those seen in Oppositional Defiant Disorder.

> Physical aggression is common. Children or adolescents with this disorder usually initiate aggression, may be physically cruel to other people or to animals, and frequently deliberately destroy other people's property (this may include fire-setting). They may engage in stealing with confrontation of the victim, as in mugging, purse-snatching, extortion, or armed robbery. At larger ages, the physical violence may take the form of rape, assault, or in rare cases, homicide.

> Covert stealing is common. This may range from "borrowing" others'possessions to shoplifting, forgery, and breaking into someone else's house, building, or car. Lying and cheating in games or in schoolwork are common. Often a youngster with this disorder is truant from school, and may run away from home.

Associated features. Regular use of tobacco, liquor, or nonprescribed drugs and sexual behaviour that begins unusually early for the child's peer group in his or her milieu are common. The child may have no concern for the feelings, wishes, and well-being of others, as shown by callous behaviour, and may lack appropriate feelings of guilt or remorse. Such a child may readily inform on his or her companions and try to place blame for misdeeds on them.

Self-esteem is usually low, though the person may project an image of "toughness." Poor frustration tolerance, irritability, temper outbursts, and provocative recklessness are frequent characteristics. Symptoms of anxiety and depression are common, and may justify additional diagnoses.

But some people are more trouble to themselves than to others. Let me quote the diagnostic criteria for 301.50 Histrionic Personality Disorder:

A pervasive pattern of excessive emotionality and attention-seeking, beginning by early adulthood and present in a variety of contexts, as indicated by at least four of the following:
(1) constantly seeks or demands reassurance, approval, or praise
(2) is inappropriately sexually seductive in appearance or behaviour
(3) is overly concerned with physical attractiveness
(4) expresses emotion with inappropriate exaggeration, e.g., embraces casual acquaintances with excessive ardour, uncontrollable sobbing on minor sentimental occasions, has temper tantrums
(5) is uncomfortable in situations in which he or she is not the centre of attention
(6) displays rapidly shifting and shallow expression of emotions
(7) is self-centred, actions being directed towards obtaining immediate satisfaction; has no tolerance for the frustration of delayed gratification
(8) has a style of speech that is excessively impressionistic and lacking in details, e.g., when asked to describe mother, can be no more specific than, "She was a beautiful person".

10.2 A manual for action

I had heard the Manual being described as a great new tool for science, an important step forward, but must confess to some disappointment as to the scientific breakthroughs. When I see the details, I do not think I would feel enriched in my insights if I came across a report on persons classified as "hysteric" or suffering from "conduct disorder".

But what I can see, is that this Manual is useful for the purposes of control. With this Manual in hand, I would have little difficulty in finding suitable diagnostic categories, both for myself and for those close to me. I do not believe this is only due to personal peculiarities, or to living in a peculiar network.

The Manual offers possibilities for decisions due to its broad and imprecise categories, and particularly due to the technique of adding up these alternative criteria: if four out of eight of them are present, she or he is of a particular type... These labels, or diagnostic categories as the American Psychiatric Association would say, are of little help in gaining deep insight into the peculiarities of a particular person. To gain such insight would demand extended talk, observations and empathy, if it could be gained at all. The psychiatric labels based on the Manual are as empty as the categories derived from the sentencing table. For sentencing purposes, the label classifies the person as deserving 36 months of imprisonment. For psychiatric purposes, the label classifies the person as deserving treatment for conduct disorder.

In another way too, the Manual is comfortable for decision makers. Again we are confronted with a grading system, one which creates distance from the person to be decided on. And again we are confronted with a system suitable for computers. When, in a short interview, the necessary number of criteria is reached, the conclusion is also within reach. The Manual is not impressive scientifically. But it has potential as a most efficient management tool.

As in penal law, again, so also in psychiatry. Most of us have committed acts that might have been classified as criminal, and most of us have acted in ways that could get us diagnosed as suffering from some sort of Mental Disorder. With the usual cooperation between law and psychiatry, the totality of the control becomes perfect.

But it can't happen here?

Well, this is what Feeley (1991) describes (p. 7):

> For every offender housed in a privately managed jail or prison, there are hundreds in privately operated non-custodial treatment programs operating on contracts with state and local governments. Despite their numbers and importance, these private programs are largely ignored in discussion of privatization in corrections. This may be because such programs are regarded as merely service providers rather than penal programs. Or it may be because their role as agents of state control is obscured because participation is voluntary. But if we broaden our frame of reference and consider them as forms of punishment (or substitutes for incarceration), we must realize that these new treatment programs are also integral components of the penal system that extend the reach of the criminal sanction and expand the array of penalties the state can impose. As such, they are part of a much expanded repertoire of punishments which can be used in concert with each other. In the aggregate they also constitute an impressive extension of state control which is often exempted from due process standards required of public agencies ...

Chapter 11

Modernity and behaviour control

11.1 Children of modernity

The title of this chapter was selected with care. Its intention is to establish a link to Zygmunt Bauman's important book on *Modernity and the Holocaust* (1989).

Bauman represents the third wave in understanding the extermination camps during the Second World War.

First came the wave of explaining the camps as the product of abnormal minds. From Hitler all the way down to the guards in the camps, those who worked there were seen as deviants, mad, and of course bad, or as disturbed authoritarian personalities (Adorno et al. 1950), or at least as under command of others of that sort. How else could the horror be explained, how else could it be understood that the country of Goethe and Schiller and the most advanced of sciences went so wrong?

The second wave of explanations moved from deviant persons to deviant social systems. The atrocities had something to do with deep defects in the German nation, perhaps with peculiar political constellations, all triggered by persons of the type described in wave one, the bad or mad or deeply authoritarian people. Normal people commit abnormal acts when situations become abnormal. I have myself written in that tradition on guards in concentration camps (Christie 1951).

The third wave is radically different. Here, extermination is not seen as an exception, but as a logical extension of our major type of social organization. In this perspective, the Holocaust becomes a natural outgrowth of our type of society, not an exception to it. Extermination becomes a child of modernity, not a return to an earlier stage of barbarism. The conditions for the Holocaust are precisely those that have helped to create the industrial society: the division of labour, the modern bureaucracy, the rational spirit, the efficiency, the scientific mentality, and particularly the relegation of values from important sectors of society. In this perspective, the Holocaust is one example, but only one, of what might happen where large sectors of activities are exempted from being evaluated by the total set of values – the ordinary home-standards of decency. The commander of Auschwitz would probably not have invited his favourite aunt for a visit. One of the doctors invited his wife – to his great regrets (Lifton 1986).

Extermination camps were like blueprints of rationally organized societies. As expressed by Bauman (pp. 11–12):

> … none of the societal conditions that made Auschwitz possible has truly disappeared, and no effective measures have been undertaken to prevent such possibilities and principles from generating Auschwitz-like catastrophes.
> …
> I propose that the experience of the Holocaust, now thoroughly researched by the historians, should be looked upon as, so to speak, a sociological "laboratory". The Holocaust has exposed and examined such attributes of our society as are not revealed, and hence are not empirically accessible, in "non-laboratory" conditions. In other words, *I propose to treat the Holocaust as a rare, yet significant and reliable, test of the hidden possibilities of modern society.*

The happy optimists[1], all the believers in steady and endless progress for humanity, are not given much comfort in Bauman's book. There exists a hidden alliance of believers in progress and even more believe

---

1 Norbert Elias (1978, 1982) is often seen as one of these. His optimistic perspective is this: From living under conditions demanding a constant readiness to fight, and with free play of the emotions in defence of one's life and possessions from physical attack, we have moved into a complex society demanding civility and personal restraint. But in extreme contrast to his message stands its dedication: To the memory of his parents, dead in Breslau 1940 and Auschwitz 1941. The behaviour of – or for – states seems to a large extent to be outside of the interests of Elias in these books. For a more positive view on Elias, see Garland (1990).

in the modern "gardening state" who view society as an object for designing, cultivating and weed-poisoning. Bauman is in strong opposition to all this. He works in the tradition of Ivan Illich and the group around him – most recently manifested in the "Dictionary of Progress" (Sachs 1992). To Bauman, the Holocaust is more than its own horrors. It is also a warning sign. Up to now it is the clearest indicator that industrialization does not mean progress, that we are on the wrong track, and that the cure cannot be just getting more of the same.

Bauman warns against the Jewish tendency to monopolize Holocaust, to make it into a phenomenon peculiar to the Jews. Ivan Illich is on the same line and argues (oral comunication) that the attention given to anti-Semitism has made us blind to the more general roots of extermination. This monopolization also makes us blind to the destiny of all the other groups – gypsies, homosexuals, communists in the concentration camps – and of the supposed opponents of the Soviet-regime in the Gulags.

The central part of Bauman's explanation of Holocaust is the *social production of moral indifference in modern societies.* That indifference was created by authorization, by routinization and by dehumanization of the victims by ideological definitions and indoctrinations.

Bureaucratization was essential in this process. As stated by Hilberg in his monumental study of *The Destruction of The European Jews* (1985, vol III, p. 10 11):

> A Western bureaucracy had never before faced such a chasm between moral precepts and administrative action; an administrative machine had never been burdened with such a drastic task. In a sense the task of destoying the Jews put the German bureaucracy to a supreme test.

And they were not peculiar people. From top to bottom, they were just ordinary. Hilberg continues his point:

> Any member of the Order Police could be a guard at a ghetto or on a train. Every lawyer in the Reichs Security Main Office was presumed to be suitable for leadership in the mobile killing units; every finance expert to the Economic-Administrative Main Office was considered a natural choice for service in a death camp. In other words, all necessary operations were accomplished with whatever personnel were at hand.

Extermination was not decided on from the outset. At first, the goal was to make Germany judenfrei – free of Jews. But then Austria was added, and also had to be free of Jews. They could be dumped in the eastern territories, but local administrators protested. Madagascar was seen as a possiblility; Eichmann spent a whole year on that idea, but Britain ruled the waves, and Eichmann was ordered to change plans into physical extermination:

> The rest was the matter of co-operation between various departments of state bureaucracy; of careful planning, designing proper technology and technical equipment, budgeting, calculating and mobilizing necessary resources. ... the choice was an effect of the earnest effort to find rational solutions to successive "problems" as they arose in the changing circumstances. (Bauman pp. 16–17).

The process was not directed by monsters. It was organized by the Section of Administration and Economy. It was run with precision, and speed, and according to calculable universalistic rules. "Irrationality" was excluded throughout. People suspected of enjoying killing would most definitely be excluded.

Being so rational, the process was in harmony with basic elements of the civilizing process, a process characterized by the relentless elimination of violence from social life. Or, in an important addition by Bauman, a process characterized by the concentration of violence under state control. What takes place here also requires the silencing of morality as a major concern. Bauman says (the italics are his) (pp. 28–29):

> ... *the civilizing process is, among other things, a process of divesting the use and deployment of violence from moral calculus, and of emancipating the desiderata of rationality from interference of ethical norms or moral inhibitions*

> ... the conditions of the rational conduct of business – like the notorious separation between the household and the enterprise, or between private income and the public purse – function at the same time as powerful factors in isolating the end-orientated, rational action from interchange with processes ruled by other (by definition, irrational) norms, and thus rendering it immune to the constraining impact of the postulates of mutual assistance, solidarity, reciprocal respect etc., which are sustained in the practice of non-business formations.

To Bauman, the Holocaust was not an irrational outflow of barbarian tendencies, but a legitimate resident in the house of modernity. And I want to add. Holocaust is only a continuation of a major trend of European colonial history.

We are just now into a stream of Centennial years for several of the great European victories in Africa. The intellectual foundation for what turned into unbelievable atrocities was theories of development and the survival of the fittest. The tools for the survival of the fittest were guns against arrows. Did Hitler learn his methods from Stalin, is the theme of debate among historians and sociologists in Germany. Nonsense, says Lindqvist (1992, pp. 199–200). Hitler knew it from childhood. The air surrounding him, and also all other Europeans at the time of his youth, was saturated by the conviction that imperialism was a biological necessity leading to the inevitable extermination of the lower races. The nine year old Adolf Hitler was not in the Albert Hall on May 4 1898. It was on this great occasion - at the peak of victories in Africa - that Lord Salisbury, the Prime Minister of Great Britain, stated that the nations of the world can be divided into the dying and those alive. Hitler was not there. Even so he knew, as all Europeans knew. They knew what France had done in Africa, what England had done, and, as late-comers, what Germany had done as close to our time as 1904. Dying nations were in need of some help to get it over with.

Thus, extermination is nothing new. We should not be that shocked. Hitler's and Stalin's camps were just parts of an old tradition. But it took place inside Europe. That meant they came closer - and at the same time became more incomprehensible.

11.2 Cloth of the devil

Thoughts are unthinkable only until formulated. Here it comes:

Hitler's idea was one of Volk, of purity of the stock, and of space – Lebensraum – for the purified product. He had the capacity to realise it. The extermination camp was a product of industrialization, one product among others of a combination of thought-patterns, social organization and technical tools. My contention is that the prison system in the USA is rapidly moving in the same direction. It is also highly likely that this trend will spread into other industrialized countries, particularly in Eastern Europe. It will be more surprising if this does not take place, than if it takes place in this decade.

To some, the very idea that criminal policy in industrial democratic societies could bear the slightest resemblance to Nazi times and extermination camps sounds absurd. Most of our highly industrialised societies are democratically run, and have protection against crime as their goal, not extermination.

This is of course true. And I do not think prisons in modern industrial societies will end up as direct carbon copies of the camps. Even if the worst comes to the worst, most prisoners will not intentionally be killed in modern prison systems. A number of death sentences will be effectuated, but most prisoners will eventually be released or die by suicide, by violence during incarceration,[2] or from natural causes. Gulags are, therefore, a more relevant term for what might come than concentration camps. My gloomy suggestion is limited to saying that a large proportion of males from the lower classes may end up living their most active lives in prisons or camps. I am not even saying that this will certainly happen, but the chances are not small. Industrial progress and civilization have no built-in guarantees against such a development.

On the contrary, we can see energetic first beginnings, in the changes in the legal apparatus, in the ideology of just deserts, in the growth and efficiency of the controlling forces, in the increased numbers of prisoners, and also in the rationale for handling these prisoners. Malcolm Feeley (1991b, pp. 66–67) talks about "the new penology". By this he means a penology which is not oriented towards individuals, and particularly not towards changing these individuals through rehabilitation or punishment, but instead focuses on management of aggregate populations.

---

2 Human Rights Watch (1992) reports (p. 38) that assassination by fellow inmates has been the second or third leading cause of death in state prisons over the past ten years or so, with the first cause being illnesses and other natural causes, and suicides and inmate-to-inmate homicides alternating in second place.

The task is managerial not transformative.

…

The tools for this enterprise are "indicators", prediction tables, classification schemes in which individualized diagnosis and response is displaced by aggregate classification systems for purposes of surveillance, confinement, and control.

A central feature of the new penalty is the replacement of moral or clinical descripion of the individual with an actuarial language of probabilistic calculations and statistical distributions applied to populations.

To Feeley, this new penal policy is neither about punishing, nor about rehabilitating individuals at fault. It is instead about identifying and managing unruly groups. In our perspective in this book, just what is needed in the control of the dangerous classes. And greatly helped in performing the task by the distance created through the new penology; from individuals to categories, from morality to management and actuarial thinking.

If we want to control the Devil, we must know him. We must understand the general principles behind what happened in Germany – and preferably also in the USSR – and then try to translate those principles into whatever is relevant to an understanding of our own situation here and now.

But the Devil has his tricks. He changes his costumes. If we want to unmask the Devil, we have to see him as a general category, and on that basis understand how he will appear next time.

A first step towards such an understanding is to look out for major strains and tensions in our present structure and ask: How do these more important problems in our industrialized nations manifest themselves?

Hitler purified the stock and saw a need for Lebensraum. The superindustrialized states have the two problems we have already pointed out: first, to find lebensraum for their products; second, a solution for those no longer needed when the efficiency of the machinery increases.

And here comes the unpleasant observation: We have seen that prisons are most helpful with both problems. In the most stable of welfare states, strict penal action against the most provocative non-contributors gives room for a policy of welfare for the remainder. In other industrialized nations, imprisonment means control of the dangerous classes. But in addition, and of increasing importance, comes the fact that the whole institution of crime control in itself is a part of the system of production. The system is of great economic interest to both owners and workers. It is a system of production of vital importance to modern societies. It produces control. In this perspective, the problem arises: when is enough, enough? There is a built-in drive for expansion in industrialization. What will happen to criminal policy if the industrial development continues?

11.3 Limits to growth?

There are no "natural limits" in this area. There are no limits on raw materials, or green movements creating trouble for the industry. We are all sinners before God, and most of us have committed acts for which we could have been brought before state authorities, had there been sufficient interest in penalising us. However that may be, it is quite clear that a much greater part of the population than the present catch could be drawn into the net, if it were made sufficiently strong and fine-meshed to hold them.

Sufficient reason for stopping the expansion of the prison system could be found if industrial development as a whole came to a halt. That would shatter the dream of free enterprise. Many who had never been near the poverty line would experience that unemployment was not necessarily a result of lack of initiative, idleness, or a hedonistic life-style. The flow of money for the control industry would also dry up. Taxpayers' money – from the few who would have anything to pay – would have to be reserved for even more essential needs.

However, a deep recession is also a situation in which prisons may be seen as the most essential of all needs. In a deep recession, the dangerous class increases in size, and becomes more dangerous than ever before. As we have seen, the lower classes are already massively over-represented in all prison systems we know of.

There are no natural limits. The industry is there. The capacity is there. Two-thirds of the population will have a standard of living vastly above any found – for so large a proportion of a nation – anywhere else in the world. Mass media flourish on reports on the dangers of the crimes committed by the remaining one-third of the population. Rulers are elected on promises to keep the dangerous third behind bars. Why should this come to a stop? There are no natural limits for rational minds.

The driving forces are so overwhelmingly strong. The interests behind them are in harmony with basic values. They are morally so solidly founded. Why should they not, in the foreseeable future, succeed completely?

Germany was able to do it, to reach a final solution in the middle of a war, despite the urgent need to make alternative use of its railways as well as of the guards. The USSR was able to develop the Gulags in the midst of preparations for war, and to run them during and after it. They were not only able to do so, but benefited from the arrangements. Why should not modern, industrialized nations be even more successful?

Hitler and his people were facing a close to impossible task. So were the leaders of the USSR. How much easier will it not be to manage the new dangerous classes?

The ground has been prepared. The media prepare it every day and night. Politicians join ranks with the media. It is impossible politically not to be against sin. This is a competition won by the highest bidder. To protect people from crime is a cause more just than any. At the same time, the producers of control are eagerly pushing for orders. They have the capacity. There are no natural limits. A crime-free society is such a sacred goal for so many, that even money does not count. Who asks about costs in the middle of a total war? Management stems from the word ménage. The master model manager is the man with the whip, driving his horses around the ring. The success of management is related to its ability to simplify value structures. This condition seems to be fulfilled in modern society.

11.4 Industrialized killing

German industry was most helpful in realizing the "final solution". For extermination a gas was used called Zyklon. The gas had to be bought from private firms. According to Hilberg (1985, p. 886), the enterprises that furnished it were part of the chemical industry, specializing in disinfecting buildings, barracks and clothes in specially constructed gas chambers. The company that developed the gas method was the Deutsche Gesellschaft für Schädlingsbekämpfung – DEGESCH. The firm was owned by three corporations: I.G.Farben (42.5 per cent), Deutsche Gold- und Silber-Scheideanstalt (42.5 per cent) and Goldsmidt (15 per cent). The profit in 1942 was 760,000 Reichsmark.[3] Business went on as usual until late in the war. One plant was bombed and heavily damaged in March 1944. At this time, the SS was making preparations to send 750,000 Jews to Auschwitz, then the only killing centre still in existence. But TESTA made it once more. 2,800 kgs of Zyklon were shipped to Auschwitz. According to Hilberg (p. 891), the firm "hurriedly inquired who was to be billed". The supply was kept up to the very end.

I.G Farben participated in producing the gas for Auschwitz. But it was not certain they knew what they were doing. The sales of Zyklon B doubled from 1938 to 1943. But the gas was also used for other purposes, particularly delousing military equipment like barracks and submarines. One ton of Zyklon was sufficient for killing one million people. In 1943, 411 tons were produced (Hayes 1987, p. 362). Therefore, the producers might have been unaware of the use of their pro-

---

3 "The Zyklon was produced by two companies: the Dessauer Werke and the Kaliwerke at Kolín. An I.G.Farben plant (at Uerdingen) produced the stabilizer for the Zyklon. Distribution of the gas was controlled by DEGESCH, which in 1929 divided the world market with an American corporation, Cyanamid. However, DEGESCH did not sell Zyklon directly to users. Two other firms handled the retailing: HELI and TESTA. The territory of these two corporations was divided by a line... (this) gave to HELI mostly private customers and to TESTA mainly the governmental sector, including the Wehrmacht and the SS."

ducts in the extermination of humans. None of the leaders of I. G. Farben was later made responsible for this aspect of the atrocities.

But they had to breathe while visiting their factories. One site was next to Auschwitz. The camp provided the slave-workers for the construction work. Even the top-executives could not escape the "pervasive stench emanating from the crematoria of Auschwitz and Birkenau". The stench "simply overwhelmed the official explanation that the camps' continuous battle with typhus forced the burning of dead bodies". (Hayes 1985, p. 364). Moreover, the slave-workers were well aware of the destiny prepared for them. Supervisors from I.G.Farben "not only spoke openly of the gassing, but wielded it as an incentive to work harder". In some mines close by, also run by I.G.Farben, the conditions were even worse. Food was better, but the life expectancy in these mines dropped to somewhere between four and six weeks.

Five leaders of I.G.Farben were sentenced after the war for their use of slave-labour. The punishments were light, and some of the reasons given by the court are of relevance to the discussion of private prisons:

> we cannot say that a private citizen shall be placed in a position of being compelled to determine in the heat of war whether his government is right or wrong, or, if it starts right, when it turns wrong (Quoted in Hayes, l985, p. 332).

In 1951, the last of the leaders of I.G.Farben were out of prison. Thereafter, they all returned to prominence and prosperity as advisers or officers in numerous German corporations. And why not, asks Hayes (1985 p. 380 and 382):

> Farben's leaders chose to behave in this situation like businessmen, not revolutionaries
> …
> Their sense of professional duty encouraged them to regard every issue principally in terms of their special competences and responsibilities, in this case, to their fields and stockholders. In obeying this mandate, they relieved themselves of the obligation to make moral or social judgments or to examine the overall consequences of their decisions.

11.5 Medicalized killing

It cannot happen here. We live in democracies. We know more. Our populations have much higher levels of general education. Most importantly, we have moved into societies which are greatly influenced by the highest professional standards.

Yet those of us who have worked with problems concerning the concentration camps remain unimpressed or, worse still, filled with the deepest distrust.

What happened back in the days of extermination was precisely that the professionals did the job, in beautiful cooperation with the bureaucracy.

Scientists were essential participants. The most basic idea was purification of the stock. The not-so-pure ought not to produce children, the pure ought to produce many. Sterilisation of the unwanted and a productivity bonus to the pure followed. Those were not deviant thoughts. US scientists reported home, with envy, how ideas of race hygiene, ideas also valid in the USA, were actually being tried out in Germany.

But some unwanted people continued to appear, like the physically handicapped. They were seen as having "lives not worth living", and in a secret decree euthanasia was authorised. As the war approaches, the criteria for those to be killed widened from physical defects into mental ones. First, this was limited to the seriously mentally handicapped, then the not so seriously retarded were included, then the insane, then the psychopaths, the homosexuals, and, as cases beyond discussion in all these categories, anybody with the wrong racial background. Perfect tools were developed. Ordinary shooting proved expensive and caused the killers mental strain. Injections were less efficient than poisonous fumes from car engines. But insecticides in the form of gas proved best of all, and were accordingly used.

Doctors were essential. Medical analogies were used all the time. The German nation was seen as a body. That whole body had to be treated. When a part is sick, surgery is needed. Jews were cancer – the need to cut off the infected part of the social body was obvious. It was not killing, it was treatment. Doctors translated theory into action, and reported back to the theoreticians. They were in positions to act in person, simply by virtue of being doctors. Medicalized killing is what Lifton (1986) calls it. He interviewed twenty-nine men who had been significantly involved at high levels with Nazi medicine. Five had worked in concentration camps. He also interviewed former Nazi nonmedical professionals of some prominence. And lastly, he interviewed eighty former Auschwitz prisoners who had worked on medical blocks. More than half of them were doctors. A major finding in this study is the importance of medical thinking both in preparing the whole operation, and also in the concrete actions of extermination. Even on the railway-platforms, where the trains from the ghettos arrived, doctors were always present. There, on the spot, they decided on the concrete cases of surgery on the national body; a nod to the left – immediate extermination, a nod to the right – a sort of life in the camp for forced labour. If there were no doctors available, a dentist would do, or a pharmacist. It was important not to give ground on this point: it had to be a medical decision. Without doctors, or those close to them, on the platform, it would have been killing.

The worst nightmare will never materialize. The dangerous population will not be exterminated, except for those killed by capital punishment. But the risks are great that those seen as core members of the dangerous population may be confined, warehoused, stored away, and forced to live their most active years as consumers of control. It can be done democratically, and under the strict control of the legal institutions.

11.6 Legalized killing

– if the Holocaust was a child of industrialized society,
– if rational bureaucratic methods were a major condition for getting it all done,
– if scientific theories played an important part,
– if medical thinking was another essential condition for doing the unthinkable,

– then, there is every reason to expect similar phenomena to re-appear, if the time is ripe and the essential conditions are there.

Are they?

The industrialized societies are there, more than ever, and are also under more strain than ever. Market economy rules the world, with an "obvious" demand for rationality, utility, and, of course, profit. The lower classes, easily transformed into the dangerous classes, are there. So are scientific theories with potential for action. Drug theories are there to the effect that certain drugs – not those already in heavy use, but some new ones – are supposed to be of such a nature that the most severe of methods of investigation and penalties are legitimate in the fight against them. And the theoreticians in criminology and law are there with a helping hand. Nobody believes in treatment any more, but incapacitation has been a favourite since the birth of the positivistic theories of crime control.[4]

---

4 The International Association of Criminal Policy. (Internationale Kriminalistiche Vereinigung) was founded in 1889. The central figure was von Liszt, insisting on helping nature to control the dangerous classes, particularly the 'incorrigible', those basic opponents of social order. Again and again, von Liszt insisted that those who could not be reformed were to be incapacitated. According to Radzinowicz (1991b) he regarded the control of this group as the central and most urgent task of criminal policy:

About seventy per cent of all prisoners were recidivists and at least half of them should be designated as 'incorrigible habitual offenders'. Against them society must protect itself and, "..as we do not wish to behead or to hang and cannot transport..", what is left is detention for life or for an indeterminate period (p.39).

... every offender convicted for the third time should be regarded as an incorrigible offender and as such should be committed to this type of quasi permanent segregation (p.40).

The Habitual Offender had to be made harmless *at his expense* (von Liszt's italics) 'not ours', writes Radzinowicz (p.40), and makes von Liszt sound highly modern.

Naucke (1982, p. 557) has this to say about the Marburger Program formulated by von Liszt:

This theory is at the disposal of those who control the penal law. The Marburger program contains no instrument to differentiate between those who ought to be offered this service, and those who ought to be denied it.

And the system of law adapts itself most beautifully to the demands of modern times. The idea of just deserts makes it possible to streamline the system, and particularly to disregard all other values than the question of the gravity of the act. The ideal of matching the gravity of a crime with a portion of pain has the consequence that all other basic values that courts traditionally have to weigh are forced out of the proceedings. What was a system of justice is converted into a system of crime control. The classical distinction between the judiciary, the executive and the legislature has to a large extent dissolved. The courts become tools in the hands of politicians or, in the most extreme cases, the judges – as well as the prosecutors – become politicians themselves. Yet this is above criticism. It has none of the grave illegalities about it that marked the Holocaust or the Gulags. Now it is democratic crime control by the voting majority. To this there are no natural limits, as long as the actions do not hurt that majority.

There are no particular reasons for optimism. There is no easy way out, no prescription for a future where the worst will not come to the worst. Working with words, I have nothing more than words to offer: Words, attempts on clarifications of the situation we are in, attempts to make visible some of the values being pushed aside in recent hectic attempts to adapt to demands that are in fashion just now. Let us look once more into the institution of justice to see if there may not after all be something of value in some of the old forms of that institution.

Chapter 12

Crime control as culture

12.1 The common core

Taiwan accepts Organs This was the headline over a little Note in *Corrections Digest*, November 27, 1991. And then follows:

> Thirty-seven organs of 14 executed Taiwan criminals have been donated for transplants, a Japanese transplant specialist on Sept.30 quoted a Taiwan surgeon as saying. Masami Kizaki, chairman of the Japan Society for Transplantation, said Chun-Jan-Lee, a professor at National Taiwan University, revealed the transplants. Dr. Lee said the condemned criminals agreed to give their hearts, kidneys and livers "to be redeemed from sin". The donors were shot dead while on respirators so their blood circulation and breathing would not stop suddenly.

Again a sort of disbelief in my own eyes. It can't be done. It just can't be! But obviously it can. It was done.

And I look around, wondering, who will take action, who will go to the barricades in protest?

The *doctors?*

Why should they protest? Some would, but not necessarily because they were doctors.

Those killed were satisfied, at least with this particular aspect. The recipients of the organs were happy. The doctors might also be happy – so much health for what otherwise would only have been waste and misery. At least this would be better than cheating Turkish labourers out of their kidneys, as in England or buying then from people in need, as in India. Some lay people may have difficulty in understanding and accepting it, but doctors are trained in rational reasoning. It is almost a miracle. A blind person may get his sight back, the husband and father with a failing heart would after transplantation live a long life with his wife and children.

Some would still not be convinced, and think that the *judges* would protest. People trained in law would not allow capital punishment to be used in this way?

That would depend on the law. There may have been no laws against it, or even more dramatically, there may have been laws encouraging the practice. If shooting sentenced people while they were in respirators was the law of the country, the judges would accept it, regardless of vague feelings of uneasiness, regardless of lay reactions, regardless of surprised questions from wives and children at home after strenuous days in courts.

Hitler had the same problem.

Ordinary people had difficulty in understanding and accepting his program for the improvement of the German nation. Serious problems appeared in the early stages of the operation. The first known and officially authorized killing of an extremely handicapped child was initiated and accepted by a father. Even then, it was kept secret. But as the program was enlarged, and the criteria for "life not worth living" were widened, there were unpleasant outbursts of protest in the German population. Relatives asked for details on why and where those close to them had died. There were also unpleasant episodes of protests from local residents close to the sites of extermination and cremation. Religious groups joined forces. This brought the program to a halt – inside Germany. But now the machinery was ready, and when the war broke out most of it was moved from Germany and into the occupied territories, enlarged, and used in the way we know so well.

What am I trying to say?

I am trying to say that Charles H. Cooley (1909,1956) is right. Cooley, that great and by now generally forgotten father of sociology in the USA, had the idea that all humans had a common ground. All humans were basically similar, not because of biology, but because they shared a basic human experience. They shared the experience of being the most vulnerable of all beings during a longer period after birth than any other beings, and of being doomed to an early death if not cared for. We all, basically, have this shared human experience. If not, we are not humans. How could it otherwise be, asks Cooley, that we can read the Greek dramas, find them relevant and important to our present lives, and understand what they are all about? As I read Cooley, he finds in this shared experience the basis of a common core in humanity, a basis of shared values and rules on how to act. We all have some common gut-feelings of right and wrong, and some common basis for sensing when impossible conflicts arise. We are all, lay as well as learned, trained in law from age zero, and have built into our minds large and often conflict-filled data-bases on moral questions for our remaining lives. A Norwegian term for this knowledge would be "folkevett" or, in a slightly more old-fashioned term, "den folkelige fornuft", a sort of intuitive common sense shared by everyone.

This view is basically an optimistic one. Those who survive childhood have been helped to do so. They have experienced at least a minimum, and in many cases a maximum of social contact and care and warmth, and have thereby also absorbed the basic rules of social life. If not, they would not have grown up. The problems are the same, everywhere. So are the stored experiences.

This common core is surprisingly resistant. Humans have experience of being social beings. It is not without reason that Durkhem (1966) has altruistic suicide as one of his major types. Humans go into death for each other. That is normal, if they are ordinary people, if altruism is necessary, and if the parties are close enough to perceive each other as human beings. But this last point on closeness is important and relevant to us all. Most of us have also limits to our obligations. That is necessary for survival. We are all trapped in the old ethical dilemma: how can I eat when I know that people, right now, less than 6 hours' flight away, are starving to death? I eat, and survive.

So did, for a while, the Jewish police in the ghetto of Lodz. This ghetto was the largest in the Eastern occupied territories. Lodz was an old, highly industrialized city, a sort of Manchester of Poland. M.G. Rumkowski, the Eldest of the Jews and with absolute power inside the ghetto, had the idea that they could survive by making themselves indispensable to the German war machine. The ghetto became as one large factory, extremely well organized, with high discipline and no trouble with organized labour. Some young workers tried, but were easily pacified. But the SS-officers were never completely satisfied. Inside the barbed wire fence, the ghetto had largely independent self-government. But the Germans inspected. They saw very old people around, and small children, non-productive consumers, and ordered them out of the ghetto, to a "more comfortable place" in the country-side. Some accepted, until car-loads of used clothes came back and the realities of that supposedly comfortable place in the countryside dawned upon the inhabitants. From then on, it became more and more difficult to fill the steadily increasing quota the SS demanded from Lodz. People tried to hide among relatives and friends. Those in hiding got no food. After a while, their relatives were also denied food. Extreme altruism was shown. When people were found, other family members – still able to work – would often refuse the privilege of staying in Lodz, and instead joined children, the sick, or parents on what they by now knew was their last journey. The police, the Jewish police, had an increasingly difficult job in detecting, arresting, and deporting all those who tried to hide, but it had to be done, if the ghetto was to survive. As a reward to the policemen, their close relatives were exempt from deportation, until, in the end, they were all sent. Rumkowski himself, and his young wife, seem to have been deported in one of the last trains out of Lodz. A newspaper came out each day in the life of the ghetto, in four copies, for the inner circle. One was preserved, and large parts are now available in an English edition (Dobrozycki 1984). Not many documents can have been published more naked in the description of the largeness of humans than this one. Nor can there be many such documents showing the other side of humanity; the possibility of total destruction under duress, when hunger, humidity, frost, and desperation destroyed everything, or where otherwise decent people lost all usual inhibitions in attempts to rescue their loved ones from deportation.

So, as we all know from our personal life, there are no absolute guarantees in that common core based on similar early experience. Often it works, in relation to those we are close to. But the core can be made irrelevant by distance, or by the extreme character of the surroundings one lives in.

Or it can be made irrelevant by professional training and practice.

This is not the place to denounce professionalism. It is a blessing to be at the receiving end of high quality professional service when that service is what we have asked for and we know we need. But a dilemma is inevitable. Professional training means long specialization. It means a purification of certain skills, but also of certain values. Long specialization means long distance from the basic core of human experience. Professionalization most often means a guarantee of a good job done in the area concerned, but reduced guarantees of attention to the totality of values, to the popular common sense. What happened to medicine in Nazi times is not so peculiar. There are no built-in guarantees.

Against this background, we may again turn our attention to law. That profession works with values. If lawyers can't be trusted, who can?

That depends on what sort of law.

It depends, first and foremost, on how close that law is to the core of common human experience. Will it be a law with roots in these core areas, or will it be a law alienated from that area, and instead completely anchored in the needs of the nation, in the needs of the government, or in the general management of the industrial/economic establishment? Or, in a formulation suggesting what I believe is the ideal: how can one achieve the highest legal standards in all these special fields, without losing sight of the core norms and values drawn from the well of common human experience?

12.2 Where does law belong?

Dag Østerberg (1991) divides the major social institutions in society into four basic categories. One is for production, where rational goal attainment is predominant. Another is for reproductive institutions, where caring and service dominate. In a third category, we find the institutions of politics and power, and in a fourth are institutions for coordinating principles, values and ways of thinking. This last category is where cultural and scientific institutions belong, where knowledge is produced and reproduced, where the everlasting discussion takes place of how the world is to be perceived, and of the relationship between nature and humans.

And where does law belong? Hedda Giertsen (1991) discusses this problem in a paper with the title "Law as humanistic activity". Her answer is reflected in the title. Rather than considering law as belonging to power and politics, she points to the essentially humanistic aspects of taking decisions on legal questions. Law has to do with conceptualization and evaluation, works with often conflicting phenomena, and is not limited to dealing with exact weights on a one-dimensional scale.

With modernity, all this has changed. Law has been pushed in the direction of the first general class of institutions, that of production. Law is becoming an instrument of utility, removed from its proximity to the cultural institutions. Through that move, law loses essential qualities, particularly its roots in the core area of human experience.

The classification of the total set of institutions into four basic types makes it possible to see the problems of integrating elements from one major type of institution into institutions belonging to the other basic categories. Solutions in one class of institutions need not be suitable in other types. Universities cannot be run as factories (even though some chancellors try to) without some loss of imaginative and critical ability. Likewise, courts cannot function as instrumental tools for management without sacrificing their greatest strengths in the protection of values: spelling them out, evaluating them against each other, and also seeing to it that single-minded goals in some institutional settings are not given undue weight in the totality. Law as a humanistic discipline keeps contact with the deep human activities, and thereby with the common experience. With that anchorage, the judiciary is prepared to meet the unbelievable, and react instinctively, as if in the family circle at the dinner table. There may be no law against executions in respirators, but it does not sound right, and it ought to be stopped.

I remember a guest from Poland who visited our institute many years ago. It was in the worst period of oppression in the East. Prison figures were steadily increasing from the very low level they were at before the Second World War. Figures were still not being censored, and we asked our guest, Dr. Jerzy Jasinski from the Polish Academy of Science, to explain the trend. He made no mystery of it.[1] The old judges were all gone. The new ones came from the party. But it was not necessarily party politics that were behind the newcomers' more severe sentencing. It had more to do with cultural affiliation. The old ones came from the intelligentsia; they belonged, which could rightly be criticized, to a sort of cultural élite. This probably meant a lot of snobbishness – I am afraid I am now leaving what Dr. Jerzinski may have told us and going on with my own interpretations – but it also meant close contact with those Polish people who worked with the core problems of their time, from Sophocles to Dostoevsky. It also meant close contact with people who in their personal life-styles would tend to expose tendencies and dilemmas which would be kept under cover in circles closer to the centre of power. A judge solidly based in the cultural arena both in reading and in life would not so easily be trapped into the belief that those he sentenced were of a completely different breed.

Common ground across social classes can be established through recruitment from all those classes. Matters can be arranged so that judges come from all social classes, with varied ethnic backgrounds representative of the country. The danger in the process is a loss of roots. The lower-class judge may become more upper-class in his identifications than anyone born there. The only viable alternative

1 Later, in a more guarded form, the views were presented in The Polish Sociological Bulletin (Jasinski 1976).

seems to be to preserve the common ground through a deep integration of law in culture. This would mean, in training as well as in practice, a heavy emphasis on the general principles of law, and discouragement of all sorts of specialization. It would also mean an encouragement to work with core values and norms, and greater ability to balance many values, many concerns and even many institutions, and not be carried away by fast simplistic solutions.

But such actions demand strength, and judges in armour. Arrogance is one such protection. That is the irony of the situation. The most democratically recruited judge, an equal among equals, might in an unequal society be badly equipped to show independent respect for the core values. In a society with gross inequalities, it seems to be particularly important to tie the judge as closely as possible to all those other workers on symbols, on meaning, on understanding and on further development of the common core.

Adherence to the common core also demands some freedom from other authorities. A judge reduced to a functionary pushing a button to produce the right answer is very far from free.

Penal law is a legal area in particular need of an independent judiciary based in culture. Let me try to illustrate.

12.3 A suitable amount of pain

We have seen that the level of pain in society is not determined by crime, that punishment is not just a simple reaction to evil deeds, that it does not much affect the crime level where we place the punishment level, and that law is no natural instrument for management. This also sets us free from the burden of utility. Even to those who stick to utilitarian views of punishment, it becomes clear that we have a choice. To the rest of us, this has been clear all the way.

But this freedom immediately raises new problems. If punishment is not created by crime, how should we then determine the suitable amount of pain to be delivered within a particular society? We are free, but without clear guidelines. Why should we not have more people in prisons than we have at present? Why not a fifth of the male population, or a third for that matter? Why not re-introduce public flogging? And why not make extensive use of the death penalty?

It is possible to find an answer. It is possible, if we attempt to preserve the proximity between the institution of law and the other cultural institutions. A suitable amount of pain is not a question of utility, of crime control, of what works. It is a question of standards based on values. It is a cultural question.

There are two major ways of approaching this problem. One is to create penal theories based on strong unquestioned authorities. Utility theories have the State as their foundation. Most non-utility theories have scripts from God, prophets or other authorities. Their conception is one where the truth exists somewhere out there, given by absolute authority, and the task for the scholar is only to translate that truth into modern language. The non-utilitarian of this type is only a spokesman for God, exactly as the utilitarian is for the State. But even a cultural perspective can be captured by the state. Hitler himself decided on questions of art, particularly in painting and music. But other cultural expressions were also important to him. They expressed the state, and had to be decided by the state, which meant him. Franco, Mussolini and Stalin had similar inclinations.

An alternative to a conception of law as something existing, ready-made, from God or nature, is one where the basic principles of justice are there, all the time, but where the concrete formulations have to be re-created again and again. This alternative is one where justice does not consist of ready-made principles to be excavated using the methods applied in law or in the social sciences, but of common knowledge which each generation has to formulate into legal principles. This is a conception of each human being as a moral agent, and, to connect it to natural law, with each and every one of us as a prophet.

Punishment can then be seen to reflect our understanding and our values, and is therefore regulated by standards people apply every day for what it is possible and what it is not possible to do to others. These standards are in use, not just shown in opinion surveys. More than a tool for social engineering, the level and kind of punishment is a mirror of the standards that reign in a society. So the question for each and every one of us is: would it be in accordance with my general set of values to live in a state which represented me in this particular way? The National Theatre in Oslo represents me as a Norwegian. So do Henrik Ibsen and Edvard Grieg. But so does the fact that we executed 25 prisoners after the Second World War. The killing of Quisling is a part of me. So is the magnitude of our prison population which also in my country can be characterized as "An Affront to Civilized Society" (Stern 1987, pp. 1–8). But belonging to Western industrialized culture, I am of course also represented by what happens in the USA. It is in a way also a part of me that cultural relatives find it acceptable to do such things to so many fellow citizens.

It is not obligatory to have a National Theatre, or money for artists. Arguments in favour can only be based on values. To me it is right to have them; terribly expensive, but right. The same is, ultimately, behind the critique of certain forms of punishment. It does not feel right to cut fingers as punishment, not any more. We felt it was acceptable up to 1815, when it was removed as a punishment from the penal code. To me it does not feel right to have 2,500 people in prison either. We are free to decide on the pain level we find acceptable. There are no guidelines, except in values.

Those of us who work close to penal systems have special responsibilities, but not as experts. As a criminologist I feel more and more that my function is very similar to that of a book-reviewer or art critic. The script is not consistent, and can never be. The authors – the law commitee in the Storting for example – are not in a position where they will ever be able to give a plausible description, in a law, of the totality of the problem they handle. A legal system without room for manoeuvre creates scripts and performances like those one meets in totalitarian régimes. Everything is predetermined, for the benefit of the rulers.

Rulers, and, in democratic states politicians, invariably attempt to give the impression that theirs are rational tasks in a field where utility thinking is of obvious importance. Our counter-idea as cultural workers – or members of the intelligentsia as they would say in Eastern Europe – is to puncture this myth and bring the whole operation back to the cultural arena. The delivery of pain, to whom, and for what, contains an endless line of deep moral questions. If there are any experts here, they are the philosophers. They are also often experts at saying that the problems are so complex that we cannot act. We must think. That may not be the worst alternative when the other option is delivery of pain.

Chapter 13

Postscript

13.1 Years of growth

In October 1993, a meeting on penal problems was held in Ryazan[1], some hours' drive from Moscow. Several hundred Russians participated, as well as four criminologists from Western Europe. A lecture given by Y.I.Kalinin, General Director of the Russian Prison System. was important in the proceedings. *Table 13.1* is based on his lecture[2].

Table 13.1 Prisoners in Russia 1993

	Number of inmates
Pre-trial, 160 institutions:	138,000

Sentenced:
    14 Prisons
    513 Colonies
    59 Youth prisons
	574,000

Alcohol institutions:	35,600
Forest colonies:	100,000
Total number of inmates:	847,600

People waiting for trial in Russia are for the most part placed in rather old-fashioned prisons in urban areas. The conditions in these overcrowded prisons are extremely unsatisfactory. I have described them

1 Ryazan is where The Ministry of Interior in Russia runs its central high school for the education of prison officers.
2 The lecture is to be published in *Nordisk Tidsskrift for Kriminalvidenskab* 1994, no 4.

in *Chapter 5.6*. King (1994) has recently visited several of these prisons, and confirms this impression. After being sentenced, nearly all prisoners are transferred to corrective labour colonies[3]. These colonies are dormitories or barracks built along with factories. According to Western standards, conditions in the colonies are also cramped, but considerably less so than in the pre-trial prisons.

As we can see from the table, the total number of prisoners is 847,600. On a population basis of about 148 million, this gives us the figure of 573 prisoners per 100,000 inhabitants. There might be errors in this figure, but I have no reason to believe that the table is systematically misleading[4]. During a conference in Moscow the year before[5], I was presented with figures close to one million prisoners, but I am of the opinion that the difference in figures stems from including persons Western observers would not regard as imprisoned. Nonetheless, even the lowest estimate represents an exceptionally large prison population.

The size of the Russian prison population can most easily be commented on through an analysis of *Table 13.2*. Here we find prison figures from selected countries, mostly for 1979, 1989 and 1993. The leader in incarceration was the former USSR. From its maximum in the 1950s – with more than 1,400 prisoners per 100,000 inhabitants, USSR came down to 660 in 1979 and to 353 in 1989. But now the trend has changed. The figure of 573 for 1993 indicates that what is now Russia is on a steady course back to its position as a country with an exceptionally high prison population.

The USA is its only competitor in this table[6]. In contrast to Russia, we here find a prison population which is steadily growing, reaching an all-time high of 532[7] prisoners per 100,000 inhabitants in 1993.

3 The forerunners of colonies were the GULAGS, named after *Glavnoye Upravlenie Lagerei*, the Central Administration of Camps.
4 The figures from The Forest Colonies were not included in the report by Kalinin – these colonies belong to another Ministry – but I find it proper to include them here. The institutions for alcoholics are soon to be abolished, but will probably reappear as ordinary colonies.
5 The conference was arranged by the Centre for Prison Reform, an organization of former political prisoners.
6 China is not included. As stated in *Chapter 3.4*, its figures in 1992 were estimated somewhere between 400 and 550 per 100,000 inhabitants.

Table 13.2 Prison figures from selected countries 1979, 1989
          and 1993

	1979	1989	1993
USSR/Russia	660	353	573
USA	230	426	532
Poland	300	106	160
Estonia			300[1]
Lithuania			250
Czech Republic			158
Canada	100	111	125
Spain	37	80	117
Denmark	63[2]	66	67
Finland	106	68	67
Norway	44	56	62
Sweden	55	58	66
Netherlands	23	44	52[3]
Iceland		41	39

[1] Figures for Estonia and Lithuania are from 1992.
[2] Figures for Norway, Sweden, Denmark and Finland are from 1980.
[3] April 1994.

There are also other countries with a considerable number of prisoners in 1993. The Baltic countries Estonia and Lithuania are filling up
their prisons[8], and probably Latvia also. The prison population in
Poland[9] is once more climbing. The Netherlands, once the example

7 My figure is from PRI, Newsletter, Penal Reform International. Figures from
  Austin (1994) give 555 for USA, but here the Jail figures are from 1992. 532 is an
  underestimate, compared to the way we calculated the Russian figure. Statistics
  from Juvenile Facilities are not included in the US figures whereas they are in the
  Russian. If we include Juvenile Facilities in the US figures, the number of incarcerated persons per 100,000 inhabitants climbs to 569.
8 From Leps (1992). See also McMahon (1994) for an interesting description of the
  Baltic developments.
9 Jerzy Jasinski has kindly provided me with these figures.

of restraint, has doubled its prison population in this period, Spain has tripled[10]. Norway and Sweden are on their way up. Finland has succeeded in maintaining to keep at the low level it attained in 1989.

13.2 What is to come?

In *Chapter 5.6 – Traces of a future –* I conclude that at least for Russia, the reduction in the number of prisoners from 660 per 100,000 in 1979 to 353 in 1989 did not seem particularly solidly cemented. And indeed, the new growth to 573 gives no reason for optimism. On the contrary, several developments might lead to further large increases in the prison population.

First of all comes the important role the colonies have played in the Russian economy until now. The colonies have been among the best functioning parts of that economy. Here is a captive work force, sober, well ordered, working in two shifts in factories inside the same fence. As stated with pride in a colony I visited: "Had it not been for the heavy taxes we pay to the State, this colony, even with the pay to both guards and prisoners, would have shown a profit." And outside the windows of the director's office were stored the reasons for his pride: the farm machinery they produced in this colony.

These products are the pride of the colony, but also the potential danger for the whole system. Lately, they had not been able to find customers for their products. They produced for storage. Nor had they been able to find anybody who would receive their prisoners on release. Again a quotation: "In the old days, we could just tell a factory that they had to hire a prisoner who was to be released next month. Today, we have nobody to tell."

The dangers ahead in Russia are therefore two-fold. They have built up a large prison-industry which up to this point has been of considerable importance for the economy. But if privatization continues, this prison industry will probably not be able to compete. But it is

---

10 From Per Stangeland, Personal communication. The figure for 1993 is an estimate, based on figures of March 15, l993. The equivalent figure from March 1994 is 122.

exactly in this situation that the pressure to contain the unwanted parts of the population will increase rather than diminish. Russia has now adopted elements of economic thinking from the West, and a press that makes money from writing on crime, but without a safety-net to protect those falling outside the system, and also without any efficient control of the new entrepreneurs. The danger in this situation is that the prison system in Russia will have to substitute both for the regulatory system and for the absence of those elements of welfare which gradually have been established in so many western countries.

In June 1994, happened what was bound to happen. President Boris Yeltsin announced that he was preparing an urgent decree that would finally reckon with Russia's powerful mobsters – "criminal filth" he called them. According to the New York Times, June 19, 1994, the new decree :

> ..grants the police the right to detain people suspected of involvement in organized crime for up to 30 days without charges or bail, permits officials to root through the bank accounts of anyone suspected of criminal involvement without a court order or approval and allows the police to use anything they obtain in these searches in court. There is even a provision that permits the authorities to investigate anyone who has lived with a suspect for more than five years. Russia's current criminal code provides only for the use of evidence obtained in a search sanctioned by the court.

This happens at the very same moment when the colonies no longer will be able to compete with private industry. *The colonies will in this situation lose their production capacity and become camps for internment only.* Even recognizing the existence of a great amount of idealism and good intentions within the administration and staff in the Russian prison system, it is to be feared that the life situation for prisoners in these camps for internment will be deplorable.

But the situation in the USA has also dramatically changed during the last two years. The growth in the number of prisoners is unbelievable. And the prison industry senses the opportunities. During the very days in May 1994 as I was writing this Postscript, the American Jail Association arranged a training conference in Indianapolis. The industry received this invitation as a preparation for the conference:

JAIL EXPO 1994
TAP INTO THE SIXTY-FIVE BILLION
DOLLAR LOCAL JAILS MARKET

Jail Expo attendees are the decision-makers in local corrections – sheriffs, jail administrators, local elected officials, correctional officers, health care directors, food service directors, trainers, architects, engineers – people from across the nation involved in jail management issues, new trends, services, and products.

There are over *100,000* people who work in the nearly 3,400 local jails in the United States. Last year alone over *$65 BILLION* was spent in the industry. The local jail market is very lucrative! Jails are *BIG BUSINESS.*
(The emphasis is not mine.)

For those missing the conference in May, June offers new opportunities. The National Institute of Justice has this program:

LAW ENFORCEMENT TECHNOLOGY
FOR THE 21ST CENTURY

"The Less-Than-Lethal Alternative"

Conference objectives

* Increase Awareness of Law Enforcement Requirements
* Increase Understanding of the Value of Technology   Applied to Law Enforcement
* Highlight Technology Transfer Opportunities for the Defence Industrial Base
* Emphasize Opportunities for Industry in the Law Enforcement Market Place

This extreme growth in US prison figures is also probably just a beginning. Instead of recognizing how close they are to becoming world leaders in incarceration, the national self-perception seems to be that *"we are too soft on crime"*. The prevailing belief seems to be that criminals are just barely touched. If imprisoned at all, they are let out much too soon, free to continue their violent activities. But now at last, the nation has awakened. From now on, softness will come to an end:

100,000 new policemen,

Federal money for building more prisons,

Federal punishments for those States that will not build more prisons,

"three strikes and you are out" – an expression from baseball, but here with the meaning that you are out of ordinary life for ever if you are sentenced three times for what in practice might be relatively minor offences,

heavily extended use of mandatory sentences and also of death penalties.

The law-abiding society will regain control.

13.3 Brothers in incarceration

When the great Russian singer – and poet, and human being – Vladimir Vysotskij once visited the town of one of the large car-factories in his country, he had to walk down the long street from the railway station to his night quarters (Palmær 1986, p.10). As he walked along, one window after another opened, tape recorders were switched on, and his songs beamed out in full volume along the entire route. It was the home-coming of an emperor.

Vysotskij gave words to the experience of millions of Russians. He grew up close to one of the central railway stations in Moscow, *Rizjskij Vokzal*. The area was over-populated to the extreme. Up to twenty families might share one apartment and one toilet. This was the time of the big amnesties after Stalin's death. The prisoners came home. They told their tales and sang their sorrows. Vysotskij listened, and brought their words to the world.

In the 1950s, some 2.5 million prisoners were in the GULAGS of the USSR. We tend to think of them as political prisoners. GULAGS were the camps for a Solzhenitsyn, for an Irina Ratusjinskaja (1988) with "Grey is the colour of hope", and for all their like. And indeed, they formed a large contingent, the political prisoners, the "class enemies", those with the wrong opinions, wrong families, and the wrong class or connections. But then, as now, the camps would also have been for the more ordinary sorts, who under more ordinary conditions are put in ordinary prisons, mental hospitals or youth institutions. These were the people who – if they were permitted to return home after the amnesties – went home to Moscow or St.Petersburg, and moved in among those others at the bottom of the social system.

These must have been the same sort of people as those who now come home from the prisons and camps in the USA. Home to the inner cities of Washington, Baltimore, Los Angeles.. Among the poor, few families in Moscow would be without members with experience of life in the camps. Among the poor in the inner cities of the USA, the situation must be the same. In both nations, this will be a breeding ground for another culture. For Vysotskij and his less famous equals in Russia. For ICE-T and his equals in the USA.

Vysotskij's songs have the melancholy of Russia. Their equivalents from the USA sound to my ears more pulsating, fast, aggressive. I am not sufficiently tuned into the US-rap-arena to analyse similarities and dissimilarities in the music from Moscow/St.Petersburg versus Los Angeles/New York. A superficial impression is that Vysotskij's songs are more sad, without hope, but sometimes with strong themes of rebellion as in his famous "The Wolf Hunt". These political messages seem less clear in the US equivalents. But some of the themes are much the same: despair, distance from loved ones, friendship, ecstasy, with tragedy as the inevitable outcome.

Rightly, they are male songs. In both countries, most prisoners are males. More than 500 per 100,000 inhabitants in both these countries are now in prison – this means that at least one percent of the male population in both Russia and the USA are there. And these males are not selected at random. Most citizens from both nations will not have former prisoners as their associates. But for poor city dwellers, to be a prisoner, or to be surrounded by former prisoners, is a part of life, particularly if one belongs to an ethnic minority. Jerome Miller (1994, p.2) has this to say from the USA:

In 1992, the National Center on Institutions and Alternative Studies conducted a survey of young African American Males in the Washington, DC's criminal justice system. The survey revealed that on an average day in 1991, *more than four of every ten African American males ages 18–35 (who were residents of DC.) were in prison, jail, on probation or parole, on bail, or being sought on arrest warrants.*

Minimally, 70% of the young black men living in DC. would be arrested and jailed at least once before reaching age 35. The lifetime risk hovered between 80% and 90% (p.2).

A similar survey of black males in Baltimore, Maryland .. showed that *56% of all African American males ages 18–35 who resided in Baltimore City were in prison, jail, on probation or parole, on bail, or being sought on arrest warrants on any given day.*

13.4 The meaning of unwanted acts

Understanding social life is to a large extent a struggle to find out what sort of meaning the phenomena are given – and why. Are Kings the sons of God, or descendants of criminals with particular success? And the beautiful people, at the top of business or entertainment, are they there due to virtues comparable to their life-styles? Are poor people to be seen as idle drinkers, good for nothing, or as victims of social conditions outside of their control? Are inner cities places where those with no aspirations choose to flock together, or are they dumping grounds for those not given an even share of the benefits of modern societies?. Meaning given to certain phenomena have consequences for the measures chosen, just as the measures give meaning back.

The former prisoners of the Gulags had one stroke of good luck: They had prisoners among them easily seen as political. Not by the regime – by power holders they were seen as the most criminal of all, having committed crimes against the regime. But little by little, they were perceived differently. Slowly, more and more perceived it otherwise and the GULAGS gained the meaning of being work-camps for opponents to the regime. In the end, they became the very symbols of political oppression. When the political regime was slightly softened after Stalin, and also the internal regime in the Gulags softened, all living there shared some of the benefits. Those seen as the "pure" political prisoners functioned as the engine for reforms to the benefit of the many. Political reforms acquired criminal-political consequences.

But today? The political element is solidly buried. Crime has got the upper hand in the meaning given to those males who are without paid work. In Russia as in the USA. The political establishment in Russia has re-directed its attention to what has always been at the centre of Russian politics: the struggle between factions at the top of society. No great political attention is given those at the bottom, nor are there resources for social reforms. The meaning of crime, and transport to the colonies, is the only remaining alternative.

In the USA, the developments are the same. Inner cities are filled with deplorable acts – wife-abuse, selling sex, selling crack, killings. Crimes. Targets for war. But again, these phenomena could in addition and at the same time have been given alternative meanings. They might first and foremost have been seen as indicators of misery, asking for economic, educational, and treatment facilities on a scale comparable to what is invested in wars outside the national border. The fascinating question, seen from an outsider's perspective, is why the inner cities of the USA are seen as targets for war rather than targets for drastic social reform.

Already Alexis de Tocqueville observed that the democratic spirit and struggle for equality he met during his travels in the USA from 1831 on also had some potentially problematic aspects. Particularly, he feared the potential tyranny from all this equality (1990 p.231):

> For myself, if I feel the hand of power heavy on my brow, I am little concerned to know who it is that oppresses me; I am no better inclined to pass my head under the yoke because a million men hold it for me.

And he states, regarding the judiciary (p.131):

> My greatest complaint against democratic government as organized in the United States is not, as many Europeans make out, its weakness, but rather its irresistible strength. What I find most repulsive in America is not the extreme freedom reigning there but the shortage of guarantees against tyranny.

When a man or a party suffers an injustice in the United States, to whom can he turn? To public opinion? That is what forms the majority. To the legislative body? It represents the majority and obeys it blindly. To the executive power? It is appointed by the majority and serves as its passive instrument. To the police? They are nothing but the majority under arms. A jury? The jury is the majority vested with the right to pronounce judgement; even the judges in certain states are elected by the majority. So, however iniquitous or unreasonable the measure which hurts you, you must submit.

Russia and the USA. Two great nations. One solution.

13.5 The brakes are gone

Some will say, this cannot continue. It will be too expensive and therefore will have to come to a stop.

I doubt it. Who considers money in the midst of war? The war on drugs, the war on violence, the war on pornography, – the urgent need for safe streets and property, these are archetypical situations where money is not allowed to reign.

The particular danger in this situation is that developments in the USA might reinforce what happens in Russia. Criticism directed towards the increasing number of prisoners in Russia can easily be met with a "look to America".

This situation might also have consequences for the remaining industrialized world. When the USA breaks away from all earlier standards for what it can do against parts of its population, and when Russia regresses to its former standards, then this threatens what is usually seen as an acceptable number of prisoners in Western Europe. A new frame of reference is established. As a result, Western Europe might experience increased difficulties in preserving its relatively humane penal policies. The other countries in Eastern Europe might also feel encouraged to follow the examples of the two leaders in incarceration.

Literature

Abel, P., B. Hebenton, T. Thomas and S. Wright: The Technopolitics of Exclusion: Unpublished paper prepared for the *XIXth Annual Conference of the European Group for the Study of Deviance and Social Control.* Potsdam, Germany, 4–8 September 1991.

Adorno, T.W., Else Frenkel-Brunswik, Daniel Levinson and R. Nevitt Sanford: *The Authoritarian Personality.* N.Y. 1950.

Andenæs, Johs: Lovmotiver og strafferett. *Lov og Rett,* 1991, pp. 385–387.

Austin, James: An Overview of Incarceration Trends in the United States and Their Impact on Crime. *Paper for the National Criminal Justice Commission,* Washington 1994.

Austin, James and Aaron David McVey: The 1989 NCCD Prison Population Forecast: The Impact of the War on Drugs. *The National Council on Crime and Delinquency.* USA 1989.

Austin, James and John Irwin: Who goes to Prison? *The National Council on Crime and Delinquency.* USA 1990.

Austin, James: America's growing Correctional-Industrial Complex. *The National Council on Crime and Delinquency.* USA 1990.

Austin, James: The Consequences of Escalating the Use of Imprisonment: The Case Study of Florida. *The National Council on Crime and Delinquency,* USA 1991.

Balvig, Flemming: *Mod et nyt kriminologisk samfundsbillede. I. Å leve med kriminalitet.* (Towards a new Criminological Perspective on Society. I. To live with Crime). Denmark 1990.

Bauman, Zygmunt: *Modernity and the Holocaust.* G.B.1989.

Bazelon, D.L.: Missed Opportunities in Sentencing Reform. *Hofstr. Law Rev,* 1978, pp. 57–69.

Beck, Peter: Ny rapport om Gulag-fangenes tunge skjebne. (New report concerning the sad destiny of the Gulag prisoners). Aftenposten, Oslo, June 14, 1992.

Blumstein, Alfred: Demographic Factors: Now and in the Future. In: Growth and Its Influence on Correctional Policy. *Guggenheim Criminal Justice Program*, Berkeley, USA 1991.

Breivik, Ivar: *Lecture on Welfare Problems in Norway.* Oslo 1991. NIBR, Box 44, Blindern, Oslo 3.

Brydensholt, Hans Henrik: En Europeisk Rapport om Ledelse af et Fængselsvæsen og af Fængslingsinstitutioner. *Nordisk tidsskrift for kriminalvidenskab, 1982,* pp. 198–207.

Bureau of Justice Statistics Bulletin: *Prisoners in 1990.* U.S. Dep. of Justice 1991.

Bureau of Justice Statistics Bulletin: *Jail Inmates in 1990.* U.S. Dep. of Justice 1991.

Bureau of Justice Statistics: *National Update,* January 1992, Vol 1, No.3.

Bødal, Kåre: 350 narkoselgere (350 Drug Dealers). Oslo 1982.

Christie, Nils: *Fangevoktere i konsentrasjonsleire.* (Guards in Concentration Camps.) *Nordisk Tidsskrift for Kriminalvidenskab* 1952, Vol 41, pp. 439–458 and 1953, Vol 42, pp. 44–60. As a book, Oslo 1972.

Christie, Nils: *Unge norske lovovertredere.* Oslo 1960.

Christie, Nils: Conflicts as Property. *British Journal of Criminology 1977,* 17. pp. 1–15.

Christie, Nils: *Limits to Pain.* Oxford 1981.

Christie, Nils: *Hvor tett et samfunn?* (How tightly knit a Society?) Oslo 1982.

Christie, Nils: *Beyond Loneliness and Institutions. Communes for Extraordinary People.* Oslo 1989.

Christie, Nils: Prisons as self-expressions. In: *The Meaning of Imprisonment,* July 1989, at Bishop Grosseteste College. Lincoln 1990, pp. 2–9.

Cohen, Stanley: *Visions of Social Control.* Oxford 1985.

Cohen, Stanley: On Talking about Torture in Israel. *Manuscript 1992.*

Cooley, Charles H.: *Social Organization: A Study of the Larger Mind.* USA (1909) 1956.

Cunningham, William C., John J. Strauchs and Clifford W.Van Meter: Private Security: Patterns and Trends. *National Institute of Justice. Research in Brief.* August 1991.

Dahrendorf, Ralf: *Law and Order.* The Hamlyn Lectures. London 1985.

Dobroszycki, Lucjan: *The Chronicle of the Lódz Ghetto.* 1941–1944. Yale 1984.

Domenach, Jean-Luc: *Chine: l'archip oublié.* France 1992.

Downes, David: *Contrasts in Tolerance. Post-War Penal Policy in The Netherlands and England and Wales.* Oxford 1988.

DSM-III – *Diagnostic and Statistical Manual of Mental Disorders.* USA 1987.

Durkheim, Emile: *Suicide. A study in Sociology.* N.Y. 1966.

Elias, Norbert: *The Civilizing Process.* Vol I, *The History of Manners.* N.Y. 1978. Vol II *State Formation and Civilization.* Oxford 1982.

Ericson, Richard V., Maeve W. McMahon and Donald G. Evans: Punishing for Profit: Reflections on the Revival of Privatization in Corrections. *Canadian Journal of Criminology,* 1987, Vol. 29, No 4, pp. 355–387.

Feeley, Malcolm: The New Penology. Reformulating Penal Objectives and Implications for Penal Growth. In: Growth and Its Influence on Correctional Policy. *Guggenheim Criminal Justice Program,* Berkeley, USA 1991b.

Feeley, Malcolm M.: The Privatization of Prisons in Historical Perspective. *Criminal Justice Research Bulletin.* Sam Houston State University 1991a, vol.6 No.2 pp. 1–10.

Foucault, Michel. *Madness and Civilization.* London 1967.

Foucault, Michel: *Discipline and Punish.* The Birth of the Prison. G.B. 1977.

Foucault, Michel: *The Order of Things. An Archaeology of the Human Sciences.* London 1970.

Freeman, Richard B.: Crime and Unemployment. pp. 89–106, in Wilson, James Q.: *Crime and Public Policy.* USA 1983.

Fridhov, Inger Marie: I all stillhet. En beretning om hvordan det oppleves å vente på å bli satt i fengsel. Mimeographed, *Institute of Criminology,* Oslo 1988.

Gardner, Sir Edward: Prisons – An alternative Approach. In: Farrell, Martin: Punishment for Profit. *Institute for the Study and Treatment of Delinquency.* London 1989.

Garland, David: The punitive mentality: Its socio-historic development and decline. *Contemporary Crises.* 1986, Vol 10, pp. 305–320.

Garland, David: *Punishment and Modern Society.* Oxford 1990.

Getty, J. Arch, Gábor T. Rittersporn, and Viktor N. Zemskov: Victims of the Soviet Penal System in the Pre-war Years: A first Approach on the Basis of Archival Evidence. *American Historical Review,* October 1993.

Giddens, Anthony: *The Constitution of Society.* Oxford 1984.

Giddens, Anthony: *The Nation – State and Violence.* Cambridge 1985.

Giertsen, Hedda: *On Giving Meaning to Murder.* Lecture, University of Torino, May 1991.

Gilinsky, Yakov: Penitentiary Policy in Russia. *International Conference. Prison Reform in the Former Totalitarian States.* Moscow 1992.

Gusfield, Joseph R.: *Symbolic Crusade. Status Politics and the American Temperance Movement.* USA 1963.

Haan, Willem de: Abolitionism and Crime Control: A Contradiction in Terms. In Stenson, Kevin and David Cowell: *The Politics of Crime Control.* London 1991.

Hayes, Peter: *Industry and Ideology. I.G.Farben in the Nazi Era.* Cambridge USA 1987.

Helsinki Watch, A Division of Human Rights Watch: *Prison conditions in the Soviet Union. A Report of Facilities in Russia and Azerbaidzhan.* N.Y. 1991.

Hilberg, Raul: *The Destruction of the European Jews.* Vol I-III, N.Y. and London 1985.

Home Office: *Crime, Justice and Protecting the Public. The Government's Proposals for Legislation.* Cm 965, London, HMSO 1990.

Hulsman, Louk: Criminal Justice in the Netherlands. *Delta. A Review of Arts, Life and Thoughts in the Netherlands,* 1974, pp. 7–19.

Hulsman, Louk: The Decriminalization. *Centro Nazionale di Prevenzione e Difesa Sociale,* Bellagio, 1973, pp. 1–31

Human Rights Watch: *Prison conditions in the United States.* USA 1992.

Håkansson, Marianne: Brott och straff i U.S.A. år 2000. *Brå Apropå,* 15, 1989, pp. 13–15.

Illich, Ivan: *Celebration of Awareness.* A Call for Institutional Revolution. USA 1970.

Illich, Ivan: *Deschooling Society.* USA 1970.

Illich, Ivan: *Energy and Equity.* G.B. 1974.

Illich, Ivan: *Limits to Medicine.* G.B. 1976.

Illich, Ivan: *The Right to Useful Unemployment and its Professional Enemies.* G.B. 1978.

Illich, Ivan and Barry Sanders: *The Alphabetization of the Popular Mind.* USA 1988.

Illich, Ivan: Needs. pp. 88–101, in Sachs, Wolfgang, ed: *The Development Dictionary. A Guide to Knowledge and Power.* G.B and USA 1992.

Ingle, Joseph B., with a Foreword by William Styron: *Last Rights. 13 Fatal Encounters with the State's Justice.* Nashville 1990.

Jasinski, Jerzy: The Punitiveness of the Criminal Justice System. *The Polish Sociological Bulletin,* 1976, pp.43–51.

Jongman, Riekent W: *Crime as a political problem.* Manuscript, Groningen 1991.

King, Roy D.: Russian Prisons after Perestroika, End of the Gulag? *The British Journal of Criminology,* 1994, vol.34, pp.62–82.

Knepper, Paul and J. Robert Lilly: The Corrections-Commercial Complex. *Paper presented at the Academy of Criminal Justice Sciences Conference.* Nashville, Tennessee, 1991.

Lacotte, Christian,: Avrätting som affärsidé, *Apropå,* 1991, Number 4, pp. 8–10.

Ladurie, Emmanuel Le Roy: *Montaillou. Cathars and Catholics in a French Village 1294–1324.* London 1978. (In French: Montaillou: village occitan de 1294–1324. Editions Gallimard, Paris 1975)

Langbein, John H.: Torture and Plea Bargaining. *The University of Chicago Law Review.* 1978–79, vol 46, pp. 3–22.

Lifton, Robert Jay: *The Nazi Doctors. Medical Killing and the Psychology of Genocide.* USA 1986.

Lea, John and Jock Young: *What is to be Done about Law and Order?* G.B. 1984.

Leps, Ando: A Brief Survey of the Criminogenic Situation in the Republic of Estonia, 1945–1992. Tallinn: *The Estonian State Police,* November 1992, p. 10.

Lindqvist, Sven: *Utrota Varenda Jävel.* Sweden 1992.

Lilly, J. Robert and Paul Knepper: Toward an International Perspective on Privatization in Corrections. *Paper presented at the 1991 British Criminology Conference.* York 1991.

Logan, Charles: *Private Prisons. Cons and Pros.* New York and Oxford 1990

Lång, K.J.: Upplever fängelsesstraffet en renässans? Spekulationer om frihetsstraffets framtid. *Nordisk Tidsskrift for Kriminalvidenskab,* 1989a, Vol 110, pp. 83–94.

Lång, K.J.: Vankiluku – kriminaalipolitiikan tulosmittari (The number of prisoners as an indicator of the performance of the crime control system). In *"Rikosoikeudellisia kirjoitelmia VI-juhlakirja."* Suomalainen Lakimiesyhdistys. A-sarja 185. Vammala 1989b, pp. 271–297.

McMahon, Maeve: Crime, Justice and Criminology in the Baltics: Reflections ona Symposium. *Manuscript,* 1994.

Mauer, Marc: Americans Behind Bars: A Comparison of International Rates of Incaraceration. *The sentencing project.* Washington 1991.

Mauer, Marc: Americans Behind Bars: One Year Later. *The sentencing project.* Washington 1992.

Mann, Coramae Richey: The Reality of a Racist Criminal Justice System. *Criminal Justice Research Bulletin,* Vol.3 No.5, 1987, pp. 1–5.

Mathiesen, Thomas: *The Politics of Abolition: Essays in Political Action Theory.* Oslo 1974.

Mathiesen, Thomas: *Prison on Trial. A Critical Assessment.* London 1990.

Messinger, Sheldon and John Berecochea: Don't Stay Too Long But Do Come Back Soon. Reflections on the Size and Vicissitudes of California's Prisoner Population. In: Growth and Its Influence on Correctional Policy. *Guggenheim Criminal Justice Program,* Berkeley, USA 1991.

Milgram, Stanley: Some Conditions of Obedience and Disobedience to Authority. *Human Relations,* 1965, pp. 57–75.

Miller, Jerome G. African American Males in the Criminal Justice System. Excerpted from *Search and Destroy: African American Males In The Criminal Justice System.* To be published by Cambridge University Press in 1994.

Mitford, Jessica: *The American Prison Business.* G.B. 1974. Published in USA 1971 as *Kind and Usual Punishment.*

Morén, Kikki: Den europeiske festning? – asylpolitikk og politisamarbeid mot 1992. *Institutt for kriminologi,* 1991.

Myrdal, Gunnar: *An American Dilemma.* vol 1, USA 1964.

Naucke,Wolfgang: Die Kriminalpolitik des Marburger Programms 1882. *Zeitschrift für die gesamte Strafrechtswissenshaft.* Vol.94, pp. 525–564, 1982.

Novak, Michael: Mediating Institutions: The Communitarian Individual in America. *The Public Interest.* 1982, Vol 68, pp. 3–20.

Nozick, Robert: *Anarchy, State and Utopia.* Oxford 1974.

Ocqueteau, Frédéric: How far can Crime Prevention and Detection Sevices be Privatised? *Collected Studies in Criminological Research,* Vol XXVII, Council of Europe. Strasbourg 1990.

Pallmær, Carsten och Ola: *Vladimir Vysotskij. Sånger* 1959–80, Stockholm 1986.
Pepinsky, Harold E. and Paul Jesilow: *Myths that Cause Crime.* USA 1984.
Radzinowicz, Sir Leon and Roger Hood: The American volte-face in sentencing thought and practice. In C.F.Tapper, ed.: *Crime, Proof and Punishment. Essays in Memory of Sir Rupert Cross.* London 1981.
Radzinowicz, Sir Leon: Penal Regression: *The Cambridge Law Journal.* Vol 50, (3) 1991a, pp. 422–444.
Radzinowicz, Sir Leon: *The Roots of the International Association of Criminal Law and their Significance.* Criminological Research Reports by the Max Planck Institute for Foreign and International Penal Law, Freiburg, Germany, Volume 45,1991b.
Ratusjinskaja, Irina: *Grey is the Colour of Hope.* USA 1988.
Rawls, John: *A Theory of Justice.* Oxford 1972.
Robert, Philippe: The Privatization of Social Control. In Hood, Roger: *Crime and Criminal Policy in Europe.* Oxford 1989.
Rohn, Warren and Trish Ostroski: Checking I.D.'s. Advances in Technology Make it Easier to Monitor Inmates. *Corrections Today,* July 1991.
Rohn, Warren and Trish Ostroski: Advances in Technology Makes it Easier to Monitor Inmates. *Corrections Today,* 1991, July, pp. 142–145.
Rosenthal, Uriel and Bob Hoogenboom: Some fundamental Questions on Privatisation and Commercialisation of Crime Control, With special Reference to Developments in the Netherlands. *Collected Studies in Criminological Research,* Vol XXVII, Council of Europe, Strasbourg 1990.
Rutherford, Andrew: *Prisons and the Process of Justice.* The Reductionist Challenge. London 1984.
Rutherford, Andrew: *Growing Out of Crime. The New Era.* G.B. 1992.
Sachs, Wolfgang: *The Development Dictionary. A Guide to Knowledge as Power.* G.B. and USA 1992.
Scherdin, Lill: "Sprøyten som språk. Injeksjons-sprøyten i et kontrollpolitisk perspektiv." *Institute of Criminology,* University of Oslo 1990.
Shaw, Stephen: Penal Sanctions. Private Affluence or Public Squalor? In Farrell, Martin: Punishment for Profit. *Institute for the Study and Treatment of Delinquency.* London 1989.
Shearing, Clifford D. and Philip C. Stenning: *Private Policing.* USA 1987.
Simmel, Georg: The Metropolis and Mental Life, and The Stranger. Both in: *The Sociology of Georg Simmel.* Translated, edited and with an introduction by Kurt H. Wolf, USA, 1950. pp. 409–424 and pp. 402–408. Original edition: Die Grosstadt, Vorträge und Aufsätze zur Städteausstellung, Jahrbuch der Gehe-Stiftung 1903, 9, pp. 185–206 and Exkurs über den Fremden. Soziologie. Untersuchungen über die formen der Vergesellschaftung, Berlin 1968.
Smith, Albert G.: Arming Officers Doesn't Have to Change an Agency's Mission *Corrections Today,* July 1991, pp. 114–124, Vol 53, No 4.

South, Nigel: Reconstructing Policing. In: Matthews, Roger: *Privatizing Criminal Justice*, London 1989, pp. 76–106.

Spitzer, Steven: Toward a Marxian Theory of Deviance. *Social Problems*, 1974, pp.638–651.

Statistical Collection: *Crimes and other offences in the USSR 1990.* Moscow 1991.

Steenhuis, D.W., Tigges, L.C.M and J.J.A. Essers: The Penal Climate in the Netherlands. Sunny or Cloudy? *The British Journal of Criminology*, 1983, vol 23, no 1, pp. 1–16.

Stern, Vivien: *Bricks of Shame. Britain's Prisons.* G.B. 1987.

Stimson, William A.: A better Design for Safer Detention on Death Row. *Corrections Today,* July 1991, pp. 158–159 Vol 53, No 4.

Swaaningen, René van, John Blad and Reiner van Loon: A Decade of Research on Norm Production and Penal Control in the Netherlands. Rotterdam 1992.

Taylor, Max and Ken Peace: Private Prisons and Penal Purpose. In: Matthews, Roger (ed): *Privatizing Criminal Justice.* G.B. 1989.

The Correctional Yearbook. Instant Answers to Key Questions in Corrections 1991. Criminal Justice Institute, N.Y. 1991.

Tocqueville, Alexis: *Democracy in America.* In: Great Books of the Western World, USA 1990.

Tonry, Michael: The Politics and Processes of Sentencing Commissions. *Crime and Delinquency.* 1991, vol 37, number 3, pp. 307–329.

Tørnudd, Patrik: Fifteen Years of Decreasing Prisoner Rates in Finland. A report presented to a Study Group from Western Australia in 1991 with a Postscript, 5 November 1993. *National Research Institute of Legal Policy Research Communications.* Tutkimustiedonantoja 8 Helsinki.

Tørnudd, Patrik: Fifteen years of Decreasing Prisoner Rates in Finland. Mimeographed. *The National Research Institute of Legal Policy,* 1991.

von Hirsch, Andrew: Construction Guidelines for Sentencing: The Critical Choices for the Minnesota Sentencing Guidelines Commission. *Hamline Law Review,* vol.5, pp. 164–215.

von Hirsch, Andrew: *Doing Justice. Report of the Committee for the Study of Incarceration.* N.Y 1976.

Vysotskij, Vladimir. *Människa-Poet-Aktør..* Moskva/Gøteborg 1991.

Weiss, Robert P.: Private Prisons and the State. In Matthews, Roger: *Privatizing Criminal Justice.* London 1989, pp. 26–73.

Wilbanks, William: The Myth of a Racist Criminal Justice System. *Criminal Justice Research Bulletin,* vol.3. No. 5, 1988, pp. 1–5.

Wolfgang, Marvin E., Arlene Kelly and Hans C. Nolde: Comparison of the Executed and the Commuted among Admissions to Death Row. *The Journal of Criminal Law, Criminology and Police Science.* 1962, Vol 53, No 3 pp. 301–311.

Young, Jock: Left Realism and the Priorities of Crime Control. In: Stenson, Kevin and David Cowell: *The Politics of Crime Control.* G.B. 1989.

Young, Jock and Roger Matthews: Rethinking Criminology: *The Realist Debate.* London 1992.

Zimring, Franklin: Correctional Growth in Context. In: Growth and Its Influence on Correctional Policy. *Guggenheim Criminal Justice Program,* Berkeley, USA 1991.

Østerberg, Dag: Universitet og vitenskap i dagens samfunn. In: Wyller, Egil A.(ed): *Universitetets idé gjennom tidene og i dag.* Oslo 1991. Also in *Samtiden,* number 3, 1991.